Hazard Mitigation:
Integrating Best Practices into Planning

James C. Schwab, AICP, Editor

TABLE OF CONTENTS

Integrating Hazards into Local Planning

We will always live on a restless planet with natural hazards covering the gamut of flood, fire, wind and earthquake. Today, more than ever, American communities know more and can do more to take actions to reduce the devastating consequences of natural hazards left unchecked. Over the last century, we have faced our threats in a number of ways. We spent billions to control those hazards we knew about, but in some cases nature reacted in ways we did not expect and ways we could not predict.

Mitigation, a cornerstone of emergency management, is defined as taking sustained actions to reduce or eliminate the long-term risks to people and property from hazards. Mitigation builds community resilience and community sustainability. When a tornado or flood is upon us, it is too late to take mitigative actions; but by taking steps to lower our risk across generations, we can ensure that our communities recover more quickly from those natural events when they do occur. Building our homes and buildings outside of high-risk flood areas; fortifying our schools and hospitals and office buildings against earthquakes; constructing safe rooms for our neighbors, our friends, and our families to shelter in during high wind events are all examples of ways planners, developers, architects, engineers, and community leaders can take those necessary and sustainable actions to protect existing and future development against natural functions of the environment and reduce the need—and cost—for response and recovery after an event occurs.

Community planners have an integral role as advocates in shaping their communities. Tools that are the mainstay of the planning professional—such as building codes, zoning, and land-use plans—are keys to mitigation. However, unless the public understands that we need to change where and how we develop and live, this work won't matter. Therefore, better communication, citizen involvement, and proactive leadership set the priorities, tone, and attitude for development decisions.

Experience has also shown that emergency managers continue to take the lead on addressing hazards in their communities. Frequently, emergency managers lead mitigation planning efforts but may not always take advantage of the unique expertise that community development or zoning officials can bring to bear in the preparation of these plans. Community planners share the responsibility to seek out their emergency management counterparts and become part of the emergency management team to jointly determine what shared values and potential solutions work best for their community.

The national emergency management system has evolved to address comprehensively at all levels protection, recovery, preparedness, response, and mitigation needs. Communities that have suffered from disasters are acutely aware that disasters are inherently local, but the regional and global impacts of a disaster can be far-reaching. This knowledge places a huge responsibility on local governments to incorporate resilience and sustainability to natural hazards into their decision making.

This report is the result of a contract between the Federal Emergency Management Agency (FEMA) and the American Planning Association (APA). In 1998, under a separate FEMA contract, APA completed the widely disseminated guide, *Planning for Post-Disaster Recovery and Reconstruction* (PAS Report 483/484). That report reflected the need for greater inclusion of hazards as a factor in local planning during a time when emergency management, in the postdisaster environment, was the primary driver of change. The practice of community planning has evolved significantly in a very short time, with sophisticated and creative results evident in hazard-prone communities throughout our nation. The case studies highlighted in the pages of this report illustrate this change. However, the basic tenets of *Planning for Post-Disaster Recovery and Reconstruction* are still widely applicable for recovery and mitigation planning efforts today.

When developing this report, there was no expectation of finding a perfect solution in any one community. Integration of hazards into local plans does not exist in one ideal template. The comprehensive plans that are the most effective are unique, living documents that evolve over time. Comprehensive planning recognizes the long-term benefits of our actions, even if the process of developing a long-term plan can be a challenge. Integrating hazards into the planning process on paper is easy; putting that integration into practice amid a myriad of local variables is much tougher. The commitment and political will to address hazards wane when the immediate threat of or response to a disaster is gone. This is our challenge to address together.

The participants who assisted with the development of this report know intuitively what integration of hazards into local planning means. As a result of the groundbreaking change in federal policy with regard to the Robert T. Stafford Disaster Relief and Emergency Assistance Act, as amended by the Disaster Mitigation Act of 2000, and the requirement for mitigation plans for federal disaster assistance, a national repository of almost 20,000 state, local, and tribal mitigation plans has been developed over the last decade. Hazard mitigation plans previously existed within only a few select states that included hazards as a component of comprehensive planning in land-use enabling laws. This report shows what can be accomplished when that integration goes beyond the minimum federal requirements.

I am extremely impressed by the ability of communities to go beyond the bare minimum in community planning to achieve true reduction of risks to their built environment, future development, and, most important, to protect the people that live in, work in, or visit them. I hope that community leaders and practicing planners with the skills, knowledge, and influence are inspired to think a little bit differently about how hazards affect their communities, and how they can help their communities become resilient and sustainable.

W. Craig Fugate, Administrator
Federal Emergency Management Agency
Department of Homeland Security

Executive Summary

This PAS Report resulted from a growing awareness by both the American Planning Association and the Federal Emergency Management Agency that effective hazard mitigation requires exploiting every opportunity a community has at its disposal to promote safe growth. This awareness has grown rapidly as a result of the experience that FEMA and communities nationwide have acquired in implementing the Disaster Mitigation Act of 2000 amendments to the Robert T. Stafford Disaster Assistance and Relief Act. Planners must be able to learn from the best practices for integrating hazard mitigation into all aspects of the local planning process. The study thus includes six major case studies from across the nation.

The report's initial chapters present a framework for understanding those case studies. Chapter 1 is a brief for expanding the role of planners in hazard mitigation, detailing the value of what they bring to the table while summarizing the roles of other actors in the process. Chapter 2 explains the often complex relationships among federal and state hazard mitigation laws and local hazard mitigation planning. Chapter 3 then details the relationships between hazard-related elements and other elements in the local comprehensive plan and discusses the various types of hazard elements prescribed in state planning legislation. Chapter 4 goes on to describe how hazard mitigation can be integrated into other types of community and regional plans—specifically, area, functional, and operational plans. Chapter 5 then offers best practices for integrating hazard mitigation into the tools for implementing local policy. It also prescribes the methodology for Safe Growth Audits.

Chapters 6, 7, and 8 each offer pairs of case studies of large, intermediate, and small town and rural jurisdictions. That division helps to show that communities large and small can use best practices for integration to achieve meaningful results in reducing losses of both life and property on account of natural hazards. Finally, Chapter 9 summarizes what the report's authors have learned about what works, what does not work, and what lies ahead for our nation's communities with regard to natural hazards. The key points of those findings are:

WHAT WORKS

- Complementary Goals and Objectives in the Local Hazard Mitigation Plan and Comprehensive Plan

- Implementing Hazard Mitigation through Government Expenditures and Development Regulations

- Documenting Existing and Predicted Future Conditions and Raising Awareness of What Can Be Done about Them

- Mutual Reinforcement Between Hazard Mitigation and Other Planning Goals

- Sustaining Leadership for Hazard Mitigation

- Strong Culture of Preparedness and Mitigation

- Using External Drivers As Leverage While Focusing on Community Needs

- Proactive Outreach and Stakeholder Involvement in Planning

WHAT DOES NOT WORK

- Procrastination

- Failure to Involve Planners in Local Hazards Planning

- Failure to Engage Public Participation or to Communicate about Hazards

- Investment in Redevelopment without Accounting for Hazards

- Failure to Use Other Plans to Address Hazards

THE ROAD AHEAD

- Learn from Disasters

- Start Change Now

- Strengthen Integration of Hazards with Other Planning Activities

- Think Linkages

CHAPTER 1

Hazard Mitigation: An Essential Role for Planners

James C. Schwab, AICP, and Kenneth C. Topping, FAICP

 One of the primary goals of planning has always been the enhancement of quality of life in our communities. Most planners practice in the firm belief that their efforts are helping to improve the lives of people in the communities they serve.

Nothing is more essential to protecting quality of life than ensuring personal safety. All other benefits or public goods that people might regard as elements of a high-quality life—aesthetics, cultural activity, peaceable civic life, prosperity—are difficult or impossible to cultivate or enjoy when personal safety is in jeopardy.

▶ DEFINITION: HAZARD
MITIGATION

What exactly is hazard mitigation? According to the website of the Federal Emergency Management Agency (FEMA), "Mitigation is the effort to reduce loss of life and property by lessening the impact of disasters. This is achieved through risk analysis, which results in information that provides a foundation for mitigation activities that reduce risk, and flood insurance that protects financial investment" (www.fema.gov/government/mitigation.shtm#1). According to the Code of Federal Regulations, "Hazard mitigation means any sustained action taken to reduce or eliminate the long-term risk to human life and property from hazards" (44 CFR 201.2). ◀

Much the same can be said about public health. Protecting public health and safety has long been enshrined as an essential justification for the use of police power at all levels of government. The role of police and fire services in protecting public health and safety is made apparent on a daily basis.

As we have learned more about the environment and the risks inherent in the forces of nature, government has acquired new responsibilities to address those risks—including not allowing development to occur in ways that would be likely to increase threats to public health and safety. This responsibility has long formed the legal, constitutional, and philosophical basis of environmental law, which has strengthened over time as scientific research has strengthened causal connections between environmental quality and public health.

In the United States, both environmental and hazards-related laws are subject to the same sorts of restraint on governmental authority that apply in many other areas of public safety. The most important restraint is the injunction against takings—the appropriation by government of private property without just compensation—in the Fifth Amendment to the U.S. Constitution. As with so many issues in the law, however, this is less a matter of absolutes than of balancing considerations. Common law has never bestowed an absolute right on property owners to do whatever they please on their own land, if for no other reason than that some things they may choose to do can pose a nuisance or danger to others. For instance, a property owner who tears down part of a coastal dune system not only may be jeopardizing the integrity of that system on his own land but, by creating a breach in the natural protection those dunes afford against coastal storms and erosion, may also be jeopardizing the safety and viability of use of many neighboring property owners and renters as well. Likewise, as Firewise Communities (2009) has noted, a landowner in the wildland-urban interface who fails to manage properly the vegetation on her own property may well be endangering not only her own property in the event of a wildfire but the property of neighbors who may as a result face the consequences of an enlarged fire. Clearly, regulating development in order to minimize risk or prevent unreasonable risks is a key function of the police power in any government that has responsibility for such decisions.

While the question of regulation is usually phrased to ask whether government is going too far in a particular case, it is also important to discuss whether government has gone far enough, particularly in situations where the danger posed by development is clear (Thomas and Medlock 2008). Whether the issue is one of properly assessing the potential for slope failure resulting in landslides, of anticipating the impact of obstructions in a floodway, or some similar failure to prevent foreseeable consequences, officials as well as developers must anticipate the possibility that victims will pursue claims based on real or perceived negligence. Those who threaten claims for takings often seek to persuade officials to loosen regulations on development with threats of lawsuits, but the opposite can be true as well—after the fact, suits for damages resulting from foreseeable consequences can also tug at the public purse. As Thomas and Medlock (2008) conclude, contemporary law supports using a preventive approach to promote the public health, safety, and welfare in the face of potential disasters. When public safety is at risk, advocates of property rights ought not to be the only people gaining the attention of local elected officials.[1]

This PAS Report is, above all else, a brief for why planners must make hazard mitigation a central consideration in the comprehensive planning process and all that flows from it. It also examines how that process can establish the framework for successful mitigation and, ultimately, greater community resilience in the face of disasters. In order to achieve these goals, planners must become familiar enough with the language and logic of natural and other hazards to assert a primary role for planning in addressing them. This report aims to establish that framework.

WHAT ROLE SHOULD PLANNERS PLAY?

The field of hazard mitigation is not unoccupied. Emergency managers, in particular, have carved out significant roles there. So have civil engineers and others involved in planning for and developing public infrastructure. There are many people and institutions with stakes in the wide range of structural and nonstructural approaches to hazard mitigation.

Nevertheless, planners' role in the process is central, and the process is less robust and less comprehensive without them. Planners typically have combinations of skills that can abet success for mitigation plans. In turn, the adoption of mitigation tools can strengthen the role of planning in both the short and long term. It is critical that planners perceive the centrality of their role in this area and use their talents to the maximum benefit of public health and safety.

Facilitating Public Participation

Most planners have at least some training in facilitating public involvement, and many have acquired considerable experience in the course of their careers. Most are well aware that planning is almost inextricably intertwined with political considerations, or what political philosophers have labeled "the art of the possible." The vagaries of local political cultures go far in explaining the wide variations in both the strength and overall focus of planning systems throughout the United States. Civic context is a major factor in successful planning.

The challenge for planners involved in integrating hazard mitigation into the planning process is to leverage an element of common cause in making the community safer and achieving reductions in losses to life and property. While these goals seem like almost unassailable public virtues, there is considerable variation in what people are willing to do to achieve those goals and how much responsibility (particularly for funding) they are willing to assign to the public sector and to which levels and agencies within it. Arguments

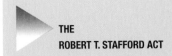

THE ROBERT T. STAFFORD ACT

The Robert T. Stafford Disaster Relief and Emergency Assistance Act (PL 100-707), signed into law November 23, 1988, amended the Disaster Relief Act of 1974 (PL 93-288). This act constitutes the statutory authority for most federal disaster response activities, especially as they pertain to FEMA and FEMA programs (www.fema.gov/about/stafact.shtm). The Stafford Act has been amended by subsequent legislation. The most notable of these for present purposes is the Disaster Mitigation Act of 2000, which for the first time tasked state and local governments with the preparation and adoption of hazard mitigation plans approved by FEMA under its implementing regulations as a condition of eligibility for receiving hazard mitigation grants from FEMA under any of several programs (see Chapter 2). This report focuses not on those plans per se but rather on the relationship of such plans to the broader comprehensive planning process and other routine planning activities at the local level.

It should be noted that while this report uses the term "local hazard mitigation plans" (LHMPs), this is a generic term for which some states use variations, such as "local mitigation strategy." All such terms, however, refer to local or tribal plans prepared to comply with the Disaster Mitigation Act and, in some cases, with complementary state or tribal laws and regulations. ◄

Figure 1.1. *A postdisaster community meeting in Greensburg, Kansas*

about relative responsibilities of local, state, and federal governments can seem endless, but they often reflect the dominant local political culture.

One vivid example comes from Louisiana, where, prior to Hurricane Katrina, levee districts had been balkanized by local considerations. One of the major reforms in the wake of that disaster was to consolidate those districts into just two authorities, one on each side of the river. The state also assumed a much larger role in planning the restoration of coastal wetlands—seen as providing some natural buffer against storm surge—than it had previously.

In this context, planners can help by initiating the public dialogue *before* disaster strikes, helping people to understand the urgency of the problem through effective public outreach and education. This entails involving as many key stakeholders as possible and helping them to achieve consensus on as many broad principles and action items as possible, given the prevailing norms of the community. The centrality of establishing planning teams and involving citizens in order to generate informed public support for a local hazard mitigation plan is a common thread in FEMA's series *State and Local Mitigation How-to Guides* (FEMA 2001–2003), a nine-volume set of CD-ROMs and publications produced to help communities after the passage of the Disaster Mitigation Act of 2000 (DMA) amendments to the Robert T. Stafford Act (see sidebar). Subsequently, requirements for public participation were written into the regulations implementing DMA (44 Code of Federal Regulations Parts 201 and 206). Public participation has long been a desideratum for most communities engaged in comprehensive planning; making mitigation a central issue in the comprehensive plan strengthens such participation in those aspects of the plan addressing local hazards.

Sometimes, however, it is necessary to conduct this discussion *after* a disaster because circumstances have left no other choice. Even then, solid community leadership can produce remarkable results, as in the commitment of citizens and local government in Greensburg, Kansas, to rebuild a "green" community after an EF-5 tornado devastated the town on May 4, 2007 (see Greensburg, Kansas + BNIM 2008; Kansas Office of the Governor and FEMA Region VII 2007).

Planning Process

Planners are versatile professionals, and the skill set required for success is quite broad. Planners' understanding of the planning process is systemic and requires knowing how to move projects, including the development of comprehensive and other types of plans, from the original goal-setting stages to completion and adoption.

This knowledge makes planners essential to hazard mitigation planning for two important reasons. First, they can aid in drafting and communicating a plan with clear goals and objectives that are in substantial agreement with the articulated goals and objectives of the community. More important, however, they should also be able to show how the goals and objectives of any hazard mitigation plan or comprehensive plan element relate to *other* existing or proposed plans and plan elements.

Comprehensive Vision and Goal Setting

The ability to integrate hazard mitigation into the larger context of plan making in a community is tied directly to another unique and crucial planner's skill: the ability to think comprehensively about the challenges facing a community, how to address them with the resources available, and how to steer the public and its decision makers toward goals and objectives that are reasonably constructed to achieve the desired ends. Many other local government professionals are trained to manage particular and often isolated functions—civil engineering with sewer and water systems, for example, or police and fire officials with public safety—but few, with the exception of county, city, or town managers, are trained to think about the welfare of the community in its entirety, with all the complex relationships that exist among land use, economic development, population growth, the environment, and the physical impact of the built environment on any number of other factors. Planners' ability to think the big, long-term thoughts about the interrelatedness and interdependency of all these factors makes them indispensable to hazard mitigation planning.

Influencing Policy

The ability to see the big picture also allows planners to function well close to power (see Lucy 1988). Local elected officials, particularly mayors, seldom have the luxury of focusing on one issue at a time. More often, they (along with county, city, or town managers) face a variety of simultaneous challenges involving budgets, tax base, development, state and federal mandates, and a host of other issues. The people they typically value most are those who can help them see around corners, anticipate consequences, and devise solutions they can sell to the public.

And yet, it has been historically difficult to sell public officials on making hazard mitigation a priority because it usually involves short-term political costs for dealing with consequences in a future beyond the term of most officeholders. At the same time, local political histories across the country are full of examples of the high price of being caught off guard, such as Jane Byrne's upset mayoral victory in Chicago in 1979 following a major snowstorm that the public did not feel was well handled by the incumbent. When a large disaster does occur, local officials often play the "blame game" out of fear of being considered having been unprepared for the crisis. Concerns about political vulnerability, therefore, are significant forces both before and after a disaster.

The ability to influence policy makers is fraught with challenges and is a product of a variety of personal and professional skills—and sometimes even the mere accident of personal relationships developed over time. Nonetheless, many planning directors have honed valuable skills that, when brought to bear on issues of hazard mitigation, should elevate the issue as a public priority in important ways.

Land-use Regulation

In most communities, planners are responsible for drafting and implementing the codes that govern land use. (Communities without permanent planning staff tend to hire planning consultants to assist with such tasks.) Planners are the one group of local government professionals specifically trained to analyze spatial relationships, plan for future growth and development, and implement the resulting decisions.

Despite this, few planners are formally trained to understand how hazards should influence those tasks and processes. The number of planning schools that incorporate such training into their curriculums is small, though growing, so many planners have essentially learned on the job or through continuing education training. Thousands of communities have by necessity learned to incorporate National Flood Insurance Program land-use requirements into their local codes, and necessity driven by experience with past disasters, sometimes coupled with state and local legislation, has compelled many others to address land-use issues connected with earthquakes, hurricanes, landslides, and whatever other hazards affect their environments.

Strategic Points of Intervention

While it may seem obvious that planners are well positioned to coordinate planning for hazard mitigation, the rationale for planner involvement in this field is more profound. What is at stake is not just one more plan or compliance with federal standards under the Disaster Mitigation Act of 2000 but the need to investigate the opportunities in every stage of the planning process—from visioning to financing to implementation—to make a community safer through cost-effective hazard mitigation. This involves identifying strategic opportunities for intervention in all of the activities in which planners are routinely involved, including:

- Visioning and goal setting for the community

- All forms of plan making, including not only the comprehensive plan but area and functional plans

- Using tools such as zoning, subdivision, planned unit development, and landscaping codes

- Reviewing and preparing development proposals, including redevelopment plans, site plan review, and development agreements

- Capital budgeting, including capital improvements programs, to ensure that public funds are invested in mitigation as needed

The remainder of this chapter will explore the roles of other professionals in this process and how planners can best relate to them in the interest of ensuring successful hazard mitigation.

WHO ELSE IS INVOLVED?

Planners often gather and synthesize information from a number of other professionals. This is especially true with hazard mitigation because it requires technical information from a number of scientific and technical sources, which vary depending on the nature of the hazards. Civil and structural engineers can provide a wealth of data, as can hydrologists, geologists, and climate and weather specialists, among others. In addition, the implementation of hazard mitigation projects can involve emergency managers, public administrators, public works officials, and others. Nevertheless, planners remain best trained to synthesize that information, structure it into plans, and outline a path to implementation. What follows is a brief summary of the roles played by some others in the hazard mitigation planning process.

Elected Officials

The legal force of most types of public plans depends on their adoption by a body of elected or appointed officials, usually the former. Under the Disaster Mitigation Act of 2000 (DMA), local hazard mitigation plans are not approved by FEMA until the plan is formally adopted by the local governing body of the jurisdiction, whether a county board, city council, or some other elected law-making entity. In most states, local comprehensive plans are official only after formal adoption by the elected governing body of a municipality or county, with only a few states authorizing final adoption by the planning commission. It stands to reason, then, that the support of elected officials is critical to the successful integration of hazard mitigation into the planning process.

This is not merely a matter of casting a vote for adoption at the tail end of the process. Mayors, city council members, county supervisors or commissioners, and other elected officials send signals on a daily basis about the level of importance they attach to various goals and objectives of local government policy. Their involvement and support can help ensure public understanding and support, just as their disinterest or outright opposition can work to doom prospects for success. Ten states have explicit mandates to local jurisdictions to include a hazards element in local comprehensive plans (IBHS 2009), but in the others it is distinctly helpful for planning commissions and their staffs to hear from elected officials that they see the use and importance of including such an element.

City and Town Managers

In many communities, city and county managers and their staffs are responsible for the professional management of local government, and they thus set the tone for many planning decisions. Like planners, they tend to see their communities in their entirety, particularly with regard to budgets and financial opportunities. Their knowledge of hazards and the degree of priority they assign to mitigation of them can make a significant difference in the success or failure of local programs.

Planning Commission Members

The planning commission usually comprises local citizens appointed by local elected officials. While many of these people are design professionals (architects, engineers, builders, etc.) with a natural interest in the subject matter, they do not necessarily know a great deal about hazards. Offering such information or including this topic in training programs can become an important task for the planning staff. A few states require a certain number of training hours for commissioners, affording some opportunity for organizations that provide such training to include at least a basic introduction to hazard-related issues in local planning and zoning (Nolon 2007).

Emergency Managers

In many states and communities, emergency managers have been given the lead role in developing local hazard mitigation plans. This occurs primarily because FEMA requirements generally are administered by emergency management agencies at the state and local levels, with the notable exception of the National Flood Insurance Program, which is handled largely by floodplain managers. This arrangement is less than ideal, however, if emergency managers fail to reach out to and collaborate with allied professions and stakeholders—as planners also need to do—to ensure a well-rounded plan with adequate provisions for implementation. Emergency managers often have considerable expertise, including knowledge of evacuation routes and plans, familiarity with emergency operations plans (for which they are primarily responsible), and understandings of a community's physical, social, and other vulnerabilities. Emergency managers are trained to observe and anticipate what might go wrong in their communities when disaster strikes and to respond quickly and efficiently with the resources available. As illustrated in the case study of Lee County, Florida (see Chapter 6), emergency managers can also serve as effective champions for integrating mitigation into comprehensive planning within their jurisdictions.

One significant advantage emergency managers have is their perspective on the comprehensive cycle of emergency management, which comprises four activity phases of mitigation, preparedness, response, and recovery (Perry and Lindell 2007, chap. 1). Ideally, emergency managers understand how these are interrelated and interdependent, with each phase blending into and contributing to better performance in the next one. This understanding of the cyclical pattern of disasters, when communicated well, can help shape wider community awareness that hazards are always present, that the next disaster is a matter of time, and that mitigation planned and implemented during the lull between events can pay serious dividends in reducing future death and destruction.

Equally important is the professional training of emergency managers to view risk from an all-hazards perspective, consistent with the goals of DMA. This allows for an effective integration of hazard information within the community, ideally with a grasp of how particular solutions can help address multiple hazards. When emergency managers work from this perspective with planners who understand multiple-objective management, in which hazard mitigation is achieved in a way that serves other public policy objectives such as environmental quality and enhancing public recreational opportunities (for example, in riverfront parks), the synergy can be both powerful in marshaling the necessary resources and politically very effective.

Emergency managers also play an important role in planning and executing evacuation plans (Schwab, Eschelbach, and Brower 2007, chap. 11). The aim of evacuation is to save lives; its viability depends on the feasibility of using planned routes. Bridges that are not high enough above flood levels or that buckle in an earthquake provide poor paths to safety, as do roads with sections that are routinely flooded. Likewise, inadequate egress from homes and subdivisions in the wildland-urban interface can leave residents trapped in a raging inferno. Addressing these issues in a mitigation plan and implementing solutions in a timely manner are crucial to protecting citizens.

There are some distinct limitations in the training of most emergency managers, however, relative to mitigation planning. Most are not necessarily familiar with the various elements of a community's comprehensive plan and are not generally engaged with planners in day-to-day operations. Emergency managers are unlikely to be trained in designing and conducting a collaborative planning process or facilitating public involvement. Their skill sets do not typically include activities related to land use and building codes but focus more often on operations planning and implementation, vehicles, machinery, and warning systems. Often, planners must help supply this larger vision.

Fire Officials

Many local fire departments in communities affected by wildfire hazards are actively involved in mitigation outreach and education activities within their communities, training neighborhood residents in firewise landscaping and vegetation management (Schwab and Meck 2005, chap. 5), as well as conducting evacuation drills.

Public Works Employees

The exact boundaries of the responsibilities of public works departments vary from one locality to another, but they almost always include water and sewer systems and often transportation system management as well. Communities with municipal electric systems may also include those under public works. In addition, public works departments often include responsibilities for urban forestry, which can become a critical response function in areas with extensive tree damage after a wind or ice storm. Mitigation functions in these cases may involve systematic programs for treating or removing hazardous street trees in order to reduce such vulnerabilities, as well as guiding choices of more resilient trees (Schwab, ed. 2009). The U.S. Forest Service (e.g., Burban and Andresen 1994) has long provided guidance with regard to mitigating the impact of storms on the health of the urban forest.

Because maintaining sewer and water services even in an emergency is essential, public works departments are critical targets for municipal continuity-of-operations plans (Perry and Lindell 2007, chap. 8). One need only consult the experience of Des Moines, Iowa, in losing its water treatment plant in the 1993 Midwest floods to gain a sense of just how critical this function can be (Schwab et al. 1998, chap. 1). While water treatment and sewage treatment plants tend to be near water bodies such as rivers for good reasons, for mitigation purposes it is also critical that they be adequately protected by floodwalls and levees. Equally important are the protection of collection and distribution systems for water and sewage, protection of lift stations, and the decentralization of water treatment facilities. These systems can be vulnerable to a number of hazards ranging from flooding and erosion to ground shaking and landslides, all of which implicate design, construction, and location decisions. In addition, public works agencies often have some responsibility for stormwater management, which also has major land-use implications.

Because of these critical, ongoing responsibilities, public works engineers can bring some of the most crucial information into the mitigation planning process. They are responsible in various ways for a significant portion of what are typically identified as "critical facilities"—those that are essential in some way to the community's ability to function and recover during and after a disaster.

Transportation Planners and Engineers

Some of the most dramatic system failures in disasters, such as the collapse of the Cypress Viaduct during the Loma Prieta earthquake, have historically involved transportation. (See Figure 1.2.) Under the stress of natural hazards, such facilities can succumb to a variety of pressures including wind, waves, storm surge, erosion, floodwaters, slope failure, and seismic shaking. Landslides, for instance, have been one focus of extensive research supported by the Transportation Research Board to identify effective mitigation techniques (see Turner and Schuster 1996).

One major opportunity for integrating hazard mitigation into transportation planning occurs at a regional level but with significant opportunity for local government input. Metropolitan planning organizations (MPOs), operating under federal transportation legislation, already produce long-range transportation plans (LRTPs). These have not typically included much if any emphasis on hazard mitigation, but they can and should. A pilot project in this area is being conducted by Florida State University's

U.S. Geological Survey Open-File Report 90-547

Figure 1.2. Reinforcement bars lie at the base of the Cypress Viaduct of Interstate 880, Oakland, California, October 17, 1989.

Department of Urban and Regional Planning in cooperation with the MPO of Charlotte County, Florida. The project is developing a set of guidelines for best practices including various analytical tools for exposure and vulnerability assessments for coastal flooding and sea-level rise, as well as evacuation scenarios (Walther 2009).

GIS Managers

Accurate and thorough mapping of hazards is critical to successful implementation of a community mitigation plan. Many communities now employ mapping specialists skilled at managing geographic information systems (GIS); these professionals can incorporate more specific risk-analysis systems, such as FEMA's HAZUS program, into broader GIS platforms in order to integrate hazard identification and risk assessment into the mapping process that supports planning. Most planners today are already familiar with GIS, and many GIS managers are trained planners, making this one of the easier arenas in which to foster collaboration.

Environmental Professionals

As the emphasis in much urban planning has shifted to sustainability, it has become apparent that environmental science will play an increasing role in helping communities identify effective means of blending environmental protection with meaningful hazard mitigation. The salience of this issue takes two critical forms. One is the role of natural systems in protecting the built environment when we allow them to perform optimally for that purpose—for example, beach and dune systems and coastal and floodplain wetlands. The other is the hideous impact that man-made environmental hazards, such as the potential release of hazardous industrial materials, can exert on exacerbating the damages inflicted on people, animals, buildings, and the natural environment during a disaster. Various types of environmental professionals, whether they are engineers, scientists, or managers, need to provide input to the hazard mitigation planning process not only in highlighting and documenting such vulnerabilities but in identifying workable solutions that can satisfy multiple community objectives.

Parks and Recreation Officials

Parks and open space have often played a critical role in the mitigation of flood hazards. Simply acquiring open space in floodprone lands can go a long way toward preventing flood damages. In Iowa City, Iowa, despite some potentially unwise development in other locations, City Park served in both 1993 and 2008 as a major retention basin for floodwaters along the Iowa River. When parks and recreation officials are brought into the process of mitigation planning, they often can help identify such opportunities as well as some nontraditional funding sources—such as parks and open space funds—that might help planners achieve their goals.

Mitigation goals related to open space often serve additional hazard-related goals. For example, Faultline Park in Salt Lake City sits on land acquired atop an earthquake fault. Other communities have acquired sensitive lands in mountainous areas that may be subject to landslides and avalanches. These areas may also host environmentally sensitive habitats for local flora and fauna that merit special protection or treatment.

Economic Developers/Business Leaders

Damage from the 1989 Loma Prieta earthquake nearly crippled downtown economic activity in Watsonville, California, for some time afterward (Eadie 1998). Downtown Cedar Rapids, Iowa, suffered for at least a year after the floods of June 2008 swamped more than 10 percent of the city (Waddington

James C. Schwab

Figure 1.3. *City Park in Iowa City, Iowa, has served as a retention basin during major floods.*

2009). Economic recovery is one of the most critical goals of hazard mitigation because without it communities lose jobs, tax revenues, and with them many of the financial resources essential to maintaining local government and facilitating rebuilding (Alesch et al. 2008). It is thus essential to involve both economic development officials and local business leaders in mitigation planning, to ensure that they are aware of the dire economic consequences of failure to mitigate and ideally to involve them as effective champions of the need for mitigation. Leaving these stakeholders outside the process only increases the likelihood that they would oppose mitigation-related expenses or regulations.

The case studies in this report bear out the effectiveness of such involvement. The desire to protect a highly vulnerable, floodprone central business district clearly drove much of the mitigation planning in Bourne, Massachusetts. In Charlotte, North Carolina, a timely invitation from local planners to developers to analyze the impact of full build-out in the floodplain under existing zoning codes produced effective buy-in for amending those codes to forestall predictable, undesirable results. Roseville, California, succeeded in involving representatives of major businesses on the steering committee for its multihazard mitigation plan, and the city's economic development team is able to market the city as a safe place to do business.

WHO SHOULD PREPARE LOCAL HAZARD MITIGATION PLANS?

While the comprehensive planning process should be the central planning tool driving hazard mitigation, most communities today prepare stand-alone hazard mitigation plans to comply with DMA; full integration of planning processes is the exception. It therefore is realistic to ask who should prepare local hazard mitigation plans. Chapter 2 will examine more closely the relationship of these federally prescribed plans to local comprehensive plans. If different players are on board for each process, integration is hard to achieve.

A recent study prepared by Boswell et al. (2008) for the California Governor's Office of Emergency Management examined the content and method of preparation of local hazard mitigation plans (LHMPs). The results do not necessarily reflect experience nationwide, but this study does provide a snapshot of hazard mitigation planning activity in a state with considerable experience in addressing natural hazards and disasters. The survey shed light on who prepares LHMPs, suggesting that local emergency managers have largely been in the lead, though planners are an important part of the team. Survey findings reveal that most plans (50 percent) were prepared in-house, 24 percent by consultants, and 18 percent by a combination of the two. (See Figure 1.4.)

Those taking the lead most frequently were first responders such as police, fire, and emergency managers (51 percent), with administrative departments a distant second. Planning and community development departments took the lead on only 8 percent of LHMPs but were considered important or very important participants in the planning process by 86 percent of those responding. (See Table 1.1.)

The question of who *should* take the lead depends a great deal on local history and leadership as well as the socioeconomic, environmental, and physical makeup of the community. Planners and emergency managers tend to have different perspectives about prospective outcomes of mitigation planning.

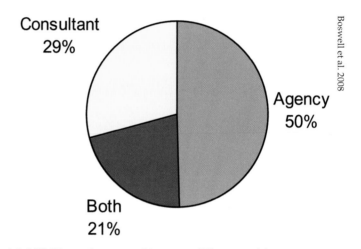

Boswell et al. 2008

Figure 1.4. LHMPs *can be prepared by many different entities.*

TABLE 1.1. PLANNING PARTICIPANTS RANKED IN ORDER OF IMPORTANCE

1. Police / Fire / Emergency Services

2. Consultants

3. Planning and Building

4. LHMP Advisory Body

5. Citizens

6. State Agencies

7. Federal Agencies

8. Special Interest Groups

9. Elected Officials

Source: Boswell et al. 2008

GUIDING PRINCIPLES

In defining the scope of this project, the American Planning Association conducted a two-day symposium in November 2007, bringing nine invited experts to Chicago as well as its own project team and mitigation staff from FEMA headquarters. The wide-ranging discussion sought to identify issues, potential case studies, and, where possible, guiding principles for planning practice. The bulleted points that follow were distilled from that discussion and, for the most part, included in a Best Practices Summary produced for FEMA review. They summarize the collective wisdom of some of the best minds in the field of hazard mitigation planning.

- *Act before a disaster.* Don't wait for Hazard Mitigation Grant Program (HMGP) funds; by the time disaster strikes, much of the damage could have been prevented through good planning.

- *Mitigation requires patience, monitoring, and continuing evaluation.* As Freudenburg et al. (2009) demonstrate in their book about the history of Louisiana's pre–Hurricane Katrina development, disasters are not built in a day. They are the product of numerous planning decisions over many years. Mitigation is often hard work that requires diligence and political patience, a key reason this report provides a new tool—Safe Growth Audits—in Chapter 5, which addresses implementation. Realize that implementation is often a messy process and develop the necessary tools to minimize vulnerability over time.

- *Be strategic and opportunistic.* Life is full of both predictable tragedy and serendipity. Disasters have silver linings. Planners who are ready when events or partnerships come along can accomplish a great deal in making their communities more secure, and they are better positioned to use fortuitous events as catalysts for change. Look for the teachable moment.

- *Champions are vital.* Political objectives need champions— either groups or individuals who will advocate for a cause. One element of seizing opportunity when it knocks is recognizing when community champions have emerged (or can be developed) who can help move the community toward embracing hazard mitigation as a strategic objective.

- *Implementation depends on political will.* It is important that planners know their local institutions in order to build crucial support for mitigation. The Disaster Mitigation Act can provide legal backbone for the process, but it is essential to do more than the bare minimum to comply. Planners can provide political cover for decision makers when implementation encounters opposition by acting as facilitators in this process.

- *Planners must account for stakeholder values in light of hazard mitigation.* They should perform an analysis of the interests of local stakeholders in order to identify both obstacles and opportunities and to compare priorities and conflicts. Involve others wherever possible.

- *Emphasize multiple-objective planning.* Drawing on such analyses, determine where the same program or objective can serve multiple purposes, such as open space and bicycle paths in a floodplain that may draw support from fitness advocates, environmentalists, and parks and recreation proponents. Find opportunities for the community to discover useful synergy in hazard mitigation.

- *Evaluate opportunities in the comprehensive plan for density reallocation.* It is possible to downzone, although timing may be key to success. The reallocation of density away from areas subject to a higher risk from natural hazards can mitigate losses in the event of a disaster.

- *Emulate the green building trend.* Why not foster a safe building trend? Why not develop new programs that embrace both greenness and safety? The Community Rating System of the NFIP—a scoring system that provides incentives for better planning—is a starting point in this direction for floodprone communities. In the same vein, modifications of the Leadership in Energy and Environmental Design (LEED) and LEED-Neighborhood Development (LEED-ND) standards could and should incorporate hazard mitigation goals.

- *Communicate risks for hazards.* Planning is not just concerned with the physical development of a community; it is also very much about public education, and planning staff must be able to communicate the elements of risk to planning commissions and the general public. The community can learn to take responsibility for the impacts of its decisions. Enabling those who wish to take foolish risks is not good planning.

- *Mitigation pays.* Part of that education is conveying the notion, persistently and convincingly, that mitigation has long-term economic benefits that have been demonstrated in credible national and local studies.

- *Above all, aim for resilience.* The long-term goal is a community with the will, the resources, and the capacity to bounce back successfully from disaster.

Planners are more inclined to look at long-term consequences of current actions in terms of the built environment, economic development, and social equity. Emergency managers tend to operate more in the present, in order to react efficiently to crises of various types. To the extent that mitigation planning influences long-term outcomes in the built environment, planners should have a strong voice in the planning process. Problems arise in situations where lack of cooperation, collaboration, and input from planners leads to mitigation actions reflecting too short-term a perspective, ignoring longer-range possibilities.

Whatever the local leadership situation, the ideal planning team includes professionals from various disciplines within local government who confer on an ongoing basis. While the California findings show that consultants are very important, where used they should be incorporated into the planning team. Turning mitigation planning entirely over to consultants may seem an easy way out to reduce workload, but it can lead to vital internal information being overlooked because consultants are typically less familiar with local circumstances.

NOTE

1. For a more extensive investigation of the law pertaining to liability for hazard mitigation, see Kusler 2009; note 143 contains a substantial list of court decisions addressing circumstances under which cities can be held liable for flood damages.

CHAPTER 2

Hazard Mitigation and the Disaster Mitigation Act

James C. Schwab, AICP, and Kenneth C. Topping, FAICP

As a societal function, hazard mitigation has been around a long time. The first known dam apparently was built nearly 5,000 years ago by the Egyptians, although it failed within a few years for lack of a watertight structure. But other ancient civilizations, including Rome and Mesopotamia, continued to experiment with better methods and materials, including concrete and clay (Yang, Haynes, Winzenread, and Okada 1999). In more recent times, hazard mitigation has been characterized by building codes, floodplain management, and other means (including dams and levees) by which people seek to protect their communities from natural forces.

The Disaster Mitigation Act (DMA) of 2000 brought hazard mitigation into clearer view and helped to define it in terms that can be understood nationwide. Preceded by a series of national laws and federal grant programs dealing with mitigation, the DMA institutionalized hazard mitigation planning both as a model process and as a condition for receipt of federal hazard mitigation grant funds by state and local governments. The overall intent of DMA is to prevent losses by building more resilient communities, and its primary tool is the use of financial incentives.

RESILIENCE

Resilience has become a topic of growing interest both academically and practically with regard to how communities fare when dealing with disasters. A number of scholars have offered definitions, including Godschalk et al. (2009):

- Instead of repeated damage and continual demands for federal disaster assistance, resilient communities proactively protect themselves against hazards, build self-sufficiency and become more sustainable. Resilience is the capacity to absorb severe shock and return to a desired state following a disaster. It involves technical, organizational, social and economic dimensions. . . . It is fostered not only by government, but also by individual, organization and business actions. ◄

HOW DMA WORKS

Mitigation has been defined by FEMA as "sustained action to reduce or eliminate long-term risk to human life and property from natural, human-caused, and technological hazards" (FEMA 2003). It is fundamentally a loss-prevention function characterized by planned, long-term alteration of the built environment to ensure resilience against natural and human-caused hazards. The loss-prevention function has been illustrated through the Multi-Hazard Mitigation Council study of FEMA mitigation projects, which showed that for every dollar invested in mitigation, four dollars of disaster losses were avoided (Rose et al. 2007).

Incentive-based Federal Legislation

Financial incentives to stimulate local hazard mitigation underlie all federal mitigation legislation, including the National Flood Insurance Act of 1968, the Robert T. Stafford Disaster Relief and Emergency Assistance Act of 1988, and the DMA.

The National Flood Insurance Act established the National Flood Insurance Program (NFIP). In 1990, through implementation of the Community Rating System (CRS), later codified in the NFIP in the National Flood Insurance Reform Act of 1994, the program established incentives for improving local floodplain management. The NFIP created a program through which federally sponsored reinsurance backed privately sold insurance, which flood victims used in recovery. The basic mitigation ingredient was federal floodplain mapping (a.k.a. Flood Hazard Boundary Maps, or FHBMs, and Flood Insurance Rate Maps, or FIRMs), together with regulations by which development was regulated within or steered away from areas susceptible to heaviest flooding. Additionally, local mitigation was promoted by establishment of the NFIP CRS program providing for graduated flood-insurance discounts in proportion to increased community flood mitigation activities that exceeded minimum federal standards. Buttressing these incentives is the Flood Mitigation Assistance (FMA) program—which offers grants for preparation of Flood Mitigation Plans, which must precede federal assistance for flood mitigation projects that may also be funded through the FMA program—as well as the Repetitive Flood Claims and Severe Repetitive Loss programs, both of which provide federal funds to help reduce losses from properties suffering repeated damage.

Experience with NFIP has been generally positive. According to the Association of State Flood Plain Managers, NFIP accounts for more than $1 billion of loss reductions annually (Larson 2003). An obvious drawback to the program, however, is that home owner participation is voluntary in most floodplain areas, thus shifting the cost burden of uninsured losses to taxpayers through higher postdisaster relief costs. The trend, however, has been to require policies where some federal "hook" is involved, such as federally backed mortgages on properties in Special Flood Hazard Areas (SFHAs). Another drawback is the mixed track record of local government compliance with NFIP standards and incentives. Some argue that NFIP has encouraged development in floodprone areas where flood risks were understated in FIRM maps (Burby 2006). Hurricane Katrina underscored the need for more accurate flood-risk assessment in levee-protected areas.

The Stafford Act, in providing the first statutory package encompassing all four basic disaster management functions—mitigation, preparedness, response, and recovery—supplied limited postdisaster funding to strengthen communities through hazard mitigation planning and projects under the Hazard Mitigation Grant Program (HMGP) as a hedge against recurrence of similar disasters in the future. In addition to a bottom-up emergency response system, by which resources are drawn from an increasingly widening area depending upon the scale of the disaster—from local to state to federal—the Stafford Act provides for three major programs: the Individual and Household Assistance (IA) program for emergency relief not offset by insurance; the Public Assistance (PA) program, which pays for 75 percent of the cost of infrastructure restoration (states and localities cover the other 25 percent); and HMGP, under Section 404. There is also an underused provision of the Public Assistance program under Section 406 authorizing additional grants for incidental costs of hazard mitigation to make infrastructure more disaster-resilient during restoration.

The essential drawback of hazard mitigation grants provided under Sections 404 and 406 of the Stafford Act is that they established mitigation as a postdisaster function—which confuses mitigation with recovery. If mitigation funding is provided only after disasters, it cannot have the same preventive value as it would before a disaster. However, in many cases the most opportune time for taking action on mitigation is after a disaster, when a community feels the most pressing need to prevent future losses. Under these programs, there is also the potentially perverse financial incentive of making the amount of HMGP funding depend on the amount of federal disaster aid received.

DMA moved beyond such limitations by creating the first nationwide stand-alone state and local multihazard mitigation planning process, yet it maintained the financial incentives approach. DMA amended the Stafford Act in two important ways: (1) it required states and localities to prepare multihazard mitigation plans as a precondition for receipt of HMGP and other federal mitigation grants, and (2) it established a competitive Pre-Disaster Mitigation (PDM) program providing for mitigation planning and project grants *before* disasters strike.

An overall purpose of DMA has been to reduce disaster losses by encouraging states, counties, cities, special districts, and tribal organizations to plan wisely for mitigating natural and human-caused hazards. Its specific intent was to make federally supported mitigation projects more effective by requiring planning in advance. A basic reason for its passage was the growing volume and severity of preventable, repetitive losses from various kinds of disasters, aggravated by the widespread occurrence of local development that ignored hazards, risk, and vulnerability issues.

The HMGP and PDM programs in particular have represented important steps triggering mitigation investments that lower future disaster losses not only after but before disaster events. Although the effectiveness of PDM has been hampered by relatively low funding levels, these two programs, together with the relatively new mitigation planning requirements, reflect a substantial national commitment to redirect disaster policy toward a more proactive stance through state and local planning initiatives. In fact, some of that commitment was already evident in prior initiatives in Florida's Local Mitigation Strategy program and North Carolina's Hazard Mitigation Planning Initiative, which provided models for the DMA rule-making process.

DMA 2000 Compliance

How well have local jurisdictions met federal standards for local hazard mitigation planning under DMA? Multihazard mitigation planning progressed slowly at first. From 2002 through 2005, FEMA published the "How To" manuals, held regional workshops for emergency managers, planners, engineers, and local officials, and enlisted the active support of State Hazard Mitigation Officers (SHMOs) from the emergency management agencies of the 50 states.

A statistical analysis of mitigation planning progress undertaken in July 2005 with available online data indicated that more than 88,000 local

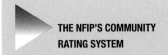

THE NFIP'S COMMUNITY RATING SYSTEM

FEMA's Community Rating System (CRS) is a voluntary program within the National Flood Insurance Program (NFIP) that allows communities to undertake activities that go beyond the minimum NFIP standards as a means of earning credits toward flood-insurance premium reductions. Points are assigned to a series of activities categorized as Public Information, Mapping and Regulations, Flood Damage Reduction, and Flood Preparedness; for each 500 points, the community earns an additional 5 percent discount for properties in Special Flood Hazard Areas (SFHAs). Communities can move from Rate Class 10, which includes all participating communities in the NFIP as well as those that have earned fewer than 500 points, through successive stages to Rate Class 1, with the highest discount of 45 percent in SFHAs. Properties in non-SFHA areas get smaller discounts of 5 percent (through Category 7) and 10 percent (through Category 1). Information on the CRS program is available at www.fema .gov/business/nfip/crs.shtm. ◀

jurisdictions, including cities, counties, special districts, and tribal organizations, were potentially eligible for HMGP and PDM project funds (Table 2.1). By then, FEMA had approved only 1,141 local plans, involving 5,763 jurisdictions, or about 6 percent of local jurisdictions nationwide. The difference in the two numbers is attributable to heavy multiagency participation in certain regions (Topping 2006).

By July 2009, more than 19,000 local and tribal jurisdictions had FEMA-approved hazard mitigation plans, representing a critical mass of new plans. As earlier, many were covered under multijurisdictional plans. These were prepared either with limited federal grant support or, more frequently, at local expense. This volume is continuing to grow and is likely to expand substantially as more jurisdictions seek eligibility for mitigation project grant funding. At the same time, many are already encountering the need to update plans as they reach the end of their five-year cycle; some may not update their plans. Local hazard mitigation plans are now required as a precondition for *all* FEMA mitigation project grants, including the HMGP, PDM, FMA, and the newer Severe Repetitive Loss and Repetitive Flood Claims programs.

State and FEMA Plan Review Processes

FEMA approval of local hazard mitigation plans under DMA 2000 involves a complex compliance review process. Each local plan is reviewed by the respective state and then by FEMA for compliance with specific items, such as hazard and risk identification, incorporation of a mitigation strategy, public and stakeholder involvement, and prioritization of mitigation actions. The process involves application of detailed requirements specified in the Code of Federal Regulations (44 CFR Part 201) and elaborated in a "Blue Book" guidance manual (FEMA 2009). Each plan is evaluated through use of a checklist, known as a "Crosswalk," by which plan content is assessed for compliance.

No systematic statistical research evaluating DMA outcomes has been undertaken nationwide. However, a survey of more than 400 local hazard mitigation plans approved by FEMA as of January 1, 2007, and representing over 500 local jurisdictions in California, provides initial insight into the character of local responses during the first round of plan preparation under DMA (Boswell et al. 2008). The picture that emerges is that of a state in which local government participation in mitigation planning is significant

TABLE 2.1. LOCAL AND TRIBAL JURISDICTIONS UNDER DMA 2000

Type of Jurisdiction	Number
Counties	3,034
Cities	19,431
Townships	16,506
Special Districts	35,356
School Districts	13,522
Native American Tribal Areas	562
Total	88,411

Sources: U.S. Census Bureau, Bureau of Indian Affairs, July 2005

and generally of good quality. Positive aspects found in most local hazard mitigation plans include the following:

- Substantive citizen participation

- Identification of hazards and consistency in prioritization of those hazards with the state perspective

- Use of the best available data on hazards from federal and state sources

- Adherence to "best practices" for vulnerability assessment (primarily FEMA "How-To" guides)

- Adoption of mitigation measures that reflect jurisdictions' hazard profiles

Moreover, the hazard mitigation planning process was viewed positively by a majority of local government respondents. (The overall response rate was 57 percent.) Overall, 85 percent of jurisdictions responding reported that preparation and adoption of the local hazard mitigation plan was either very beneficial or somewhat beneficial to the jurisdiction.

However, there were areas of concern from a general quality-control perspective. Shortcomings included the following:

- Most local hazard mitigation plans did not identify future land-use and development trends and how they affected hazards and risks, though this is a FEMA requirement.

- Most local hazard mitigation plans showed little or no connection to comprehensive general plan safety elements required under California law.

- Local hazard mitigation plans generally included a "catch-all" approach to mitigation actions, exhibited by lists of unprioritized projects dominated by emergency response and preparedness–related items rather than mitigation.

- Multijurisdictional plans indicated minimal effort by local jurisdictions to pursue mitigation measures relevant to their unique hazards and risks.

- Most important, local hazard mitigation plans had little linkage to other state or local plans.

Such issues may be addressed more fully in the next round of local hazard mitigation plan updates now under way across the nation. FEMA requires certain demonstrations of progress in the updated plans, such as how the plan was implemented and any new data or studies that might be integrated into it. During this and succeeding required updates, the opportunity exists to bring many local governments along, given sufficient clarity of communications concerning state and local integration of mitigation planning with other plans.

LINKAGES WITH OTHER PLANS

Although FEMA encouraged localities to integrate local hazard mitigation plans with other existing planning mechanisms, many approved plans appear to be largely stand-alone documents having few connections with other plans. For example, in California relatively few localities reported a connection between their local hazard mitigation plan and the adopted general plan safety element. Assembly Bill 2140, passed by the California legislature in 2006, authorizes the state to provide postdisaster financial assistance to any city or county that adopts its local hazard mitigation plan as part of the general plan safety element. However, only 12 percent of jurisdictions surveyed reported having done so. (See Figure 2.1.)

Similarly, only 10 percent reported a linkage between their local hazard mitigation plan and the 2004 California State Hazard Mitigation Plan. Table 2.2 shows the percentage of local hazard mitigation plans that link to a variety of other state and federal plans, programs, and agencies. Interestingly, the largest external link (41 percent) was with the NFIP Community

Figure 2.1. An assessment of how California LHMPs are or are not integrated with a Safety Element

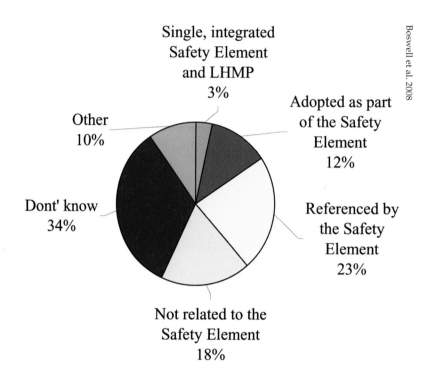

Boswell et al. 2008

TABLE 2.2. PERCENTAGE OF CALIFORNIA PLANS WITH EXTERNAL LINKS

State	
CAL FIRE	21%
State Building Code	16%
FireWise	15%
Department of Water Resources	12%
State Hazard Mitigation Plan	10%
Federal	
FEMA National Flood Insurance Program or Community Rating System	41%
Disaster Resistant Communities Initiative	0%
National Incident Management System	0%
USFS Forest Management Plan	0%

Source: Boswell et al. 2008

Rating System. Most local hazard mitigation plans had no external links at all, and 77 percent had no links to the state level.

The Problem with Stand-Alone Plans

While a stand-alone mitigation plan might be better than no plan at all, there are good reasons why local hazard mitigation plans should be linked to other community planning activities, particularly land-use planning. The most important is that, unlike the comprehensive plan, the local hazard mitigation plan has no legal status for guiding local decision making regarding capital expenditures or land use. Although the precise status of comprehensive plans varies from state to state, state courts typically find the contents of such plans persuasive with regard to the community's intent when issues arise regarding consistency of land-use regulations with the plan, and many mandate consistency (Dennison 1996). Other benefits of linkage include avoiding conflicting outcomes when plans are not coordinated and assuring improved outcomes through synchronization.

An example of a relevant conflicting outcome might be a high-density residential comprehensive plan designation on a parcel of land identified in the local hazard mitigation plan as subject to severe, repetitive flooding. Synchronization of these plans might instead lead to a very low-density residential designation for that parcel and, better yet, possible inclusion in the local hazard mitigation plan of a land acquisition program as a mitigation strategy for the general area.

Likewise, to the extent possible, local hazard mitigation plans should be coordinated with state hazard mitigation plans, particularly in terms of hazard identification and analysis and other key components. Where either state or local plans have fallen short in achieving proper linkages initially, corrective efforts should be made in successive five-year plan updates. In addition to the much larger benefit of loss prevention, other benefits that can be obtained from such state-local and internal coordination include:

- Improved pre- and postdisaster decision making at each level

- Formation of partnerships between planners and emergency managers at each level

- Expansion of external funding opportunities for state and local governments

- Facilitation of the postdisaster return to normalcy for states and communities

- Resolution of locally sensitive issues with community-based rather than externally imposed solutions

These findings reflect a clear need for encouraging (1) better integration of local hazard mitigation plans with comprehensive plans and (2) improved linkages between state and local mitigation plans. The following chapters explore the details and benefits of thorough integration throughout the planning process.

CHAPTER 3

Integrating Hazard Mitigation Throughout the Comprehensive Plan

James C. Schwab, AICP, and Kenneth C. Topping, FAICP

In planning theory, if not always in practice, the comprehensive plan—sometimes also labeled the master plan or general plan—is the central element in the community planning process. It is intended to provide a guiding vision for a community's future, to embody both the overarching public policy goals of a community and the essential reasoning behind them. It is the cornerstone upon which a community can then construct land-use controls and programs to implement its vision. This vision is important enough that all but two states either specify or suggest the specific elements that belong in such a plan. Many of these are relatively common—land use, housing, transportation, and economic development, for instance—but some arise on account of specific circumstances in a state or local jurisdiction. This chapter discusses many of the unique features of state laws that prescribe a hazards-related element in local plans. In some communities, hazards may also be addressed as part of a broader element dealing with related issues such as environmental quality, open space, or land use.

In the end, it is important both to focus on hazards in a specific element devoted to identifying and assessing the hazards a community faces and to integrate those concerns more broadly into other elements, since hazards do not operate in isolation from the built environment. They are integral—even if inimical—to all aspects of the built environment and should be addressed in an integrated context. This chapter discusses both sides of this equation in the context of the local comprehensive plan.

STATE POLICIES ON HAZARD MITIGATION AND PLANNING

The United States does not have a single common planning system for local governments to follow. While there are many federal statutes and programs that affect planning at the local level, planning and zoning power is vested in state governments, resulting in 50 systems of planning—not to mention those administered by tribal governments, the District of Columbia, U.S. territories, and the Commonwealth of Puerto Rico. Although the heritage of the model enabling acts of the late 1920s has produced common elements of planning laws in many states, significant variations among states exist today. Moreover, those model statutes were almost completely silent on issues related to natural hazards; the roles in planning for natural hazards that states have carved out simply did not exist at the time. For the most part, state roles have emerged in their current form since the creation of the NFIP in 1968 and FEMA in 1979 and, more significantly, since the passage of the Stafford Act in 1988. Nor are those roles static; they continue to change under the pressure of events, and the substantial increase in natural and human-caused disasters worldwide in recent decades has contributed an enlarged state and federal interest in mitigation.

These roles, too, must be distinct from those defined by state planning enabling laws, which tend to focus on local land-use planning and regulation, often without reference to hazards or related subjects. Beyond state planning enabling legislation, other aspects of state law and policy may play an important part, such as mapping requirements; technical assistance to local government; state emergency management law and programs; state policies on long-term community recovery; and environmental provisions with a bearing on hazards, including coastal zone management or state environmental review processes, such as the California Environmental Quality Act (CEQA). A full discussion of integration of hazard mitigation into local planning must account for the full range of state policies involved.

Moreover, recovery and mitigation are in many ways joined at the hip. Effective mitigation clearly makes recovery easier in most cases by reducing the levels of damage that occur; at the same time, the recovery period often affords significant political and financial opportunities to advance the logic of mitigation against future disasters. Thus, it should not be surprising that state policies on mitigation planning have a powerful impact on prospects for long-term community recovery, and vice versa. The U.S. Chamber of Commerce's Business Civic Leadership Center has detailed many of these interrelationships in an attempt to argue for more comprehensive state planning in this regard (Alesch n.d.).

After the passage of the Stafford Act, states prepared postdisaster mitigation plans under its Section 409 requirement to do so after receiving federal disaster assistance. More recently, both states and local governments have responded to financial incentives in DMA by developing hazard mitigation plans, the major exception being that states were given a deadline (May 2005, as extended) for submitting their initial plans to qualify for federal hazard mitigation grants. For many states, this, with some encouragement and support from local governments in developing local plans, is the extent of their policy making with regard to planning for hazard mitigation. In most cases, these are also states that take a permissive approach to local planning: They authorize it but do not require it.

Other states, however, not only require local governments to plan but require specifically that they address natural hazards in some prescribed manner within their local comprehensive plans, either with an element devoted to the topic or within one or more other designated elements. The level of detail in state guidance on this point varies widely, as do other features of state policy. APA for several years has tracked state legislation in this arena for the Institute for Business and Home Safety (2009). Two maps from that study (Figures 3.1 and 3.2) show which states require local comprehensive plans and which require hazards elements within those plans, with the latter largely overlapping the former. The exceptions are Colorado and Montana, which require such elements if a local government chooses to adopt a plan but do not require planning generally. Elsewhere, the link between mandatory local planning and mandatory hazards planning seems undeniably strong. As a general rule, so is the link between state political culture and the law of planning, although attacks on mandatory planning in Oregon and Florida in recent years suggest that those cultures can change significantly over time.

Beyond the simple considerations of mandates versus permissive authority, it is instructive to look at the specific differences in the nature and details of the mandates themselves. Schwab (2004) described a legal typology of state hazards planning mandates that, not surprisingly, followed regional lines. (See Table 3.1.)

Safety Elements and Special Hazards Laws

California, Arizona, and Nevada, with significant variations among them, have adopted state laws requiring safety elements. When adopted in 1972, the California law required both a seismic safety element for earthquakes as

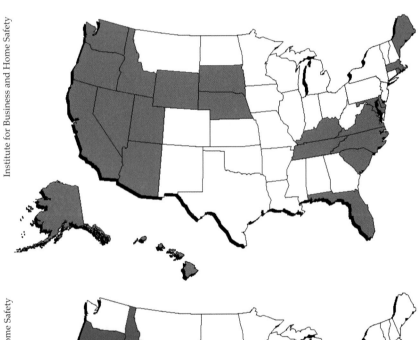

Figure 3.1. *States shown in red require some or all local governments to develop local comprehensive plans.*

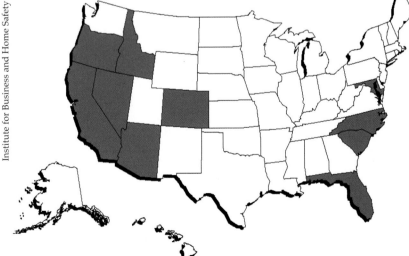

Figure 3.2. *Ten states have specific requirements that local plans must in some way address natural hazards in a specific element. The states shown here in blue do not necessarily specify the inclusion of a discrete hazards element, but they do require that natural hazards are addressed in a larger element that may address related concerns. For more information, see www.disastersafety .org/text.asp?id=building_codes.*

Institute for Business and Home Safety

Institute for Business and Home Safety

TABLE 3.1. STATE HAZARDS ELEMENT PROVISIONS

State	Code Section
Arizona	A.R.S. §9-461.05
California	Government Code §65302
Colorado	C.R.S. 31-25-206
Florida	FS 163.3177 (coastal management element)
Idaho	IS Title 67, Chapter 65
Maryland	ACM Ch. 66.B Sec.3.05(a)(4) and 3.05(a)(6)(ii)(3)
Montana	MT 76-1-6-1 and 76-5-101-110
Nevada	NS 278.160.1(k) and (l)
North Carolina	GSNC Ch. 113A-110
Oregon	ORS Chs. 197, 222, and 215
South Carolina	CSLC 48-39-250

Source: James C. Schwab

well as a safety element for all other hazards. When the California general plan law was comprehensively amended in the early 1980s, these requirements were consolidated into a single mandated safety element covering all hazards. In 2006, passage of Assembly Bill 162 added substantive new general plan law that requires inclusion of evolving federal and state floodplain mapping in land-use, housing, and conservation elements, as well as the safety elements.

Most recently, California law and policy have addressed climate change mitigation and adaptation. Under Senate Bill 375 (2008), local jurisdictions must consider development that fosters greenhouse gas reductions through regional planning, as well as implement a vigorous new state climate change adaptation strategy that stresses mitigation of flooding, wildfires, drought, heat, and other impacts. One county has already been sued successfully for a failure to consider greenhouse gas emissions in its general plan update.

Paralleling the safety element requirement in California has been a series of other laws dealing directly with mitigation measures for specific hazards, such as seismicity and wildfires, and for particular areas, such as the coast. For example, the Earthquake Fault Zone Mapping Act (1972) prohibits construction of new buildings used for human occupancy across surface traces of active faults, and Senate Bill 547 (1986) requires localities in the most seismically active areas of the state to inventory all unreinforced masonry structures and develop a mitigation program. Similarly, the Seismic Hazards Mapping Act (1990) requires mapping of areas subject to liquefaction, earthquake-induced landslides, and amplified ground shaking, and it requires geotechnical investigations before issuance of building permits in mapped zones. Additionally, Assembly Bill 304 (2005) requires inventories of soft-story buildings and authorizes adoption of local ordinances for seismic retrofits.[1] With respect to wildfire hazards, the state requires special vegetation management measures and building standards in unincorporated areas that are mapped as Very High Fire Hazard Severity Zones. However, awareness and enforcement of some of these laws are still weak.

Arizona and Nevada differ from California principally in limiting the requirement for a safety element to larger jurisdictions. Arizona specifies a safety element that includes "geologic hazard mapping in areas of known geologic hazards" for cities of more than 50,000 people. As Arizona has grown rapidly in recent decades, the number of such cities has grown apace, including, as of the 2000 Census, seven suburbs of Phoenix that each have more than 100,000 people. In Nevada, the safety plan covers a variety of natural and industrial hazards and is mandatory for counties of at least 400,000 people. A seismic safety plan is also required but is a suggested element for counties of less than 400,000.

Coastal Management Elements

Coastal management elements are required in the comprehensive plans of coastal jurisdictions in Florida, North Carolina, and South Carolina. Florida has the nation's most detailed legislation in this regard. All three states mandate these plan elements in all jurisdictions in coastal counties, but Florida's growth management system goes farther, requiring review and approval of those plans by the state Department of Community Affairs (DCA).

Florida's peninsular geography creates a situation in which tropical storms can make landfall on either the Atlantic or Gulf Coast, only to cross the state and pick up steam again over water on the other side. (Hurricanes Andrew and Katrina both crossed Florida from the Atlantic side and struck Louisiana later.) The focus of the required coastal element, however, is on evacuation and "coastal high hazard areas," which are defined in terms of hazards of storm-surge inundation. Florida has addressed wind hazards primarily through state building code amendments that materialized in the wake of Hurricane Andrew and apply statewide. However, Section 163.3177 of the Florida Statutes does encourage those "local governments that are not required to prepare coastal management elements under Section 163.3177 . . . to adopt hazard mitigation/post-disaster redevelopment plans." The policies to be included should address redevelopment, infrastructure, densities, nonconforming uses, and future land-use patterns. The same law also provides for planning grants from DCA to support preparation of such plans.

Section 163.2178 prescribes in some detail the components of a coastal management element for those coastal counties and municipalities covered by the requirement. Among those components is "a redevelopment component which outlines the principles which shall be used to eliminate inappropriate and unsafe development in the coastal areas when opportunities arise." The Florida Administrative Code provides further details and guidance for local governments as to what is expected.

Still, more than a decade passed between the enactment of these provisions and an attempt to make them a reality of local planning statewide, largely because of uncertainty about the best means of implementing the requirement for a postdisaster redevelopment plan. DCA had funded a previous assessment of the preparation of such plans and concluded that local governments needed better guidance (Deyle and Smith 1994). The state later sought funding from the National Oceanic and Atmospheric Administration (NOAA) for a pilot project to assist several jurisdictions in preparing such plans and documenting their successes and challenges. By the fall of 2008, the state developed draft planning guidelines. By early 2010, all five counties and one municipality participating in the pilot project had completed their plans (Walther 2009; Schwab 2009). One factor that the experiment underscores is the clear linkage between redevelopment after a disaster and the opportunity to implement previously considered mitigation strategies.

Aside from Florida, North Carolina and South Carolina clearly suffer the greatest frequency of disasters spawned by hurricanes along the Atlantic coast. Hurricanes Hugo in South Carolina (1988), Fran (1996) and Floyd (1999) in North Carolina, and other disasters have marked public awareness and public policy. North Carolina passed its Coastal Area Management Act (CAMA) in 1974, though this is a natural resources law rather than an amendment of planning enabling legislation. Under CAMA, local planning must address certain hazardous-area elements including coastal high-hazard areas, erosion hazard areas, and ocean-inlet hazard areas. Fundamentally, coastal area management is handled cooperatively by the state and local governments, with the Division of Coastal Management and appointed members of the Coastal Resources Commission providing standards and review, as well as planning grants, while localities take the lead in planning. The state can step in, however, and provide a plan where local governments fail to do so.

South Carolina's Beachfront Management Act dates from 1988, the year of Hurricane Hugo. (See Figure 3.3.) Under it, coastal jurisdictions are to develop a local comprehensive beachfront management plan with 10 elements specified in the act, one of which is a postdisaster plan that focuses on "cleanup, maintaining essential services, protecting public health, emergency building ordinances, and the establishment of priorities." Some permitting provisions of the act were challenged successfully before the U.S. Supreme Court in *Lucas v. South Carolina Coastal Council* (505 U.S. 1003 [1992]). Because the South Carolina Coastal Council prohibited improvements seaward of a line beyond developer David Lucas's two lots in Isle of Palms, he argued that the regulation constituted a total taking of his property, a proposition with which the court agreed, overturning the state high court and remanding the case for further hearing. The key failing was the lack of an appeal process under the 1988 law, which was amended in 1990 to address this issue. Ultimately, the state settled with Lucas and bought the lots. Not nearly as detailed or focused on redevelopment as the Florida postdisaster requirement, South Carolina's provision is nonetheless the only other state one that approximates it (Schwab 2004). However, North Carolina now encourages preparation of a redevelopment plan (particularly for any areas of severe repetitive loss) under its own local hazard mitigation planning requirements, and it has added this element as a state recommendation to the FEMA plan review crosswalk for North Carolina communities. The crosswalk is a FEMA document that allows reviewers to compare a local hazard mitigation plan's contents with official requirements in order to determine whether it is in compliance.

Figure 3.3. Damage by Hugo to South Carolina's Isle of Palms

U.S. Geological Survey

While not mandating a general plan element, passage of the California Coastal Act in 1972 has led to preparation of Local Coastal Plans (LCPs) by cities and counties along the 1,100 miles of coastline in that state. LCPs are subject to review by the California Coastal Commission, as are appeals of development projects within LCP areas. Conflicts periodically arise among the Coastal Commission, other state agencies, and local governments over environmental protection and hazards management issues.

Hazardous Areas Elements

Three Rocky Mountain states—Colorado, Idaho, and Montana—have had closely related experiences with and perspectives on the issue of treating hazards in comprehensive plans. Of the three, only Idaho requires its communities to develop comprehensive plans, but Colorado includes a hazardous areas element in the specifications for a complete plan if a local government chooses to prepare one. Not surprisingly, the common primary ingredient of disasters in these states is geological, involving varying degrees of seismic shaking and slope failure. In addition, frequent flash floods and wildfires make the case for effective hazard mitigation all the more compelling.

Idaho's Local Land Use Planning Act (Idaho Code Sec. 67-6508) describes its element as "an analysis of known hazards as may result from susceptibility to surface ruptures from faulting, ground shaking, ground failure, landslides or mudslides; avalanche hazards resulting from development in the known or probable path of snowslides or avalanches, and floodplain hazards."

Colorado uses roughly similar language requiring the delineation of sensitive areas but devotes more language to flood risks and specifically cites wildfire hazards, a regular source of concern there (Schwab 2004). Colorado also provides for two designated sources of technical assistance: the Colorado Geological Survey and the Colorado State Forest Service (IBHS 2009). The latter has been particularly active in recent years in assisting communities with the preparation of Community Wildfire Protection Plans under the federal Healthy Forests Restoration Act of 2003. What is sometimes less clear is the degree of effective collaboration on wildfire issues between local fire departments and planners.

In 2007, rising costs of fire suppression drove Montana to amend the legislation that spells out provisions for what it calls growth plans, which are primarily policy documents. Montana also does not require local comprehensive plans, but it has put certain expectations in place for those local governments that do prepare growth plans. The 2007 legislation added to those requirements "an evaluation of the potential for fire and wildland fire in the jurisdictional area," potentially including delineation of the wildland-urban interface, along with regulations for defensible space, access, and water supply and the incorporation of mitigation measures into subdivision codes.

Other Natural Hazards Planning Requirements

Two other states merit special mention: Maryland and Oregon. Both require local governments to prepare comprehensive plans, and both, in their ways, have been at the forefront of smart growth innovation through state planning policies. Maryland requires a sensitive-areas element that must include hazardous areas; Oregon uses a unique but legally powerful system of state planning goals that must be addressed in local plans, including a state goal relating to natural hazards.

Of the two, Oregon focuses considerably greater attention on the problem of natural hazards. Its planning goals and guidelines are established by the Oregon Department of Land Conservation and Development (DLCD), which reviews plans and oversees compliance. Natural hazard areas are the subject of Goal 7; they include floods, earthquakes, landslides, tsunamis, coastal erosion, and wildfires. Over the years, DLCD has published significant guidance for local governments addressing planning and mitigation options for each of these hazards. It also notifies local governments when relevant new hazard information requires a local planning response, which must occur within three years (Schwab 2004). Response includes evaluating the risk based on the new information and adopting or amending plan policies and measures to avoid both development and the siting of essential facilities in hazard areas.

The Impact of Planning Mandates

A handful of researchers have examined the efficacy of state planning mandates on loss reduction and relative safety by comparing states that mandate either comprehensive planning or hazard-related plan elements to those that do not. The consensus of their studies seems to be that such mandates do make a difference, though there is considerable opportunity to improve our understanding of just how much difference they make—and whether specifically requiring that hazards be addressed in comprehensive plans makes a bigger difference.

Burby et al. (2000), in a study predating the impact of DMA, suggested that land-use planning helps communities avoid hazards and listed a number of purposes served by such planning. They also listed state tools and training that could aid local governments in mitigating hazards and concluded with a series of principles for managing development so as to reduce local exposure to hazards, which included:

- Using maps to delineate hazards

- Preparing design guidelines for hazardous areas

- Steering development to hazard-free land

- Reviewing land for potential hazards *before* allowing subdivision

- Providing incentives for building in appropriate locations

- Purchasing properties in hazard-prone locations

- Using project-specific design to reduce hazard exposure

- Using postdisaster periods as windows of opportunity for mitigation

Burby et al. (2001) examined urban containment strategies, noting that 73 urban areas across the United States employed urban growth boundaries in efforts to reduce sprawl. They argued that such strategies can have a deleterious side effect of pushing development into increasingly hazardous areas unless accompanied by specific attention to avoiding them. Only when this was done was there evidence of an overall reduction of disaster losses.

Burby (2005) noted that three earlier studies of the 1994 Northridge earthquake had found less damage in Southern California communities that had adopted high-quality safety elements in their comprehensive plans than in those that had not. He maintained that mandates for planning tend to improve community attention to natural hazards, and he offered eight reasons why comprehensive plans tend to result in reduced exposure. He also noted the role of the "quiet revolution" of the 1970s, when several states adopted the first wave of growth management legislation, in increasing attention to hazard mitigation in comprehensive plans. He suggested that increased state provision of technical assistance for hazards planning was driven in large part by the mandates in such legislation. Most important, Burby offered the results of statistical tests on insurance losses relative to the influence of mandates, controlling for other factors; he found that states that mandated planning had lower losses overall. However, he noted the contrasting federal emphasis on single-purpose plans and hazard-specific plans. He concluded with a series of reasons for recommending comprehensive planning as the preferred tool for achieving disaster loss reduction.

Burby (2006), influenced by the tragedy of Hurricane Katrina, posed two paradoxes of national development policy with regard to hazards. First, a focus on making previously hazardous areas safe for development—such as by protecting previously flood-prone areas with levees—has tended to convert those areas into "targets for catastrophe" because increased development sets the stage for massive losses when those protective systems fail, as they did dramatically in New Orleans. Second, despite suffering losses in such catastrophes, local government tends not to pay attention to hazards, often because the losses are hypothetical until disaster strikes. Burby noted that as a result of inherent political considerations, the second paradox is more likely to change than the first, but only if the federal government helps bring about such change through policy incentives. That fact relates to a third paradox identified by Platt (1999), who noted that the federal government picks up many of the costs of disasters and remains unable to demand that local governments assume a greater share of the burden. Burby noted that almost no local flood mitigation provisions existed in local land-use codes before the creation of the NFIP in 1968 and that New Orleans provided ample examples of a failure of local government to protect its citizens by restricting hazardous development patterns.

Most recently, Deyle, Chapin, and Baker (2008) examined residential development densities in coastal high-hazard areas in Florida before and after implementation of the 1985 Growth Management Act mandates there. The act sought both to direct growth away from such areas, which must include at least a Category 1 storm-surge zone, and to maintain evacuation times within the larger hurricane vulnerability zones, which encompass Category 3 storm-surge zones. The study found "residential exposure to hurricane flood hazards to have increased substantially in the majority of 74 municipalities and 15 coastal counties after the state approved local comprehensive plans." These admittedly paradoxical results, they found, "may be due in part to vesting of development approved prior to adopting the plans, pre-existing zoning entitlements, and Florida's 1995 property rights law." If anything, this last study serves as perhaps a cautionary tale concerning expectations; implementation of even high-quality plans may sometimes have to work against the inertia of existing development patterns, including previously issued permits.

Challenges of Integrating State and DMA Requirements

The preceding discussion illustrates the varying provisions of state planning enabling statutes and special hazard mitigation laws. Chapter 2 reviewed the national standards for hazard, risk, and vulnerability assessments laid down by DMA and its implementing guidelines. Initial evidence in the California local hazard mitigation plan assessment undertaken in 2007 (Boswell et al. 2008) suggests that DMA provides a beneficial template of good practice against which state and local hazard mitigation planning can be both reasonably measured and further refined.

While systematic figures are not available, there is ample evidence that approval by FEMA of 19,000 hazard mitigation plans during the first round of local planning under DMA 2000 has generated new understandings about the reality of hazards, risk, and vulnerability that previously went unaddressed at the community level. The abiding issue lies in how to encourage integration of these efforts with ongoing state and local planning. There are still significant numbers of jurisdictions, particularly in rural areas, with no planning commissions or staff and where creating a plan to comply with the

Stafford Act DMA amendments constituted their first attempt at any kind of planning. At this point, this effort, like parallel efforts by individual states, seems to represent a positive exercise in local capacity building likely to prove generally beneficial and cost-effective when ultimately tested.

Within this overall picture, several questions have emerged:

1. How can nationwide DMA implementation be made more effective at state and local levels?

2. How can duplication of effort be avoided when implementing both federal and state mandates?

3. How can transferable best mitigation practices within individual states be identified and promoted on a nationwide level?

DMA represented a turning point in national mitigation policy, which individual states and communities can leverage to their advantage. To determine the overall costs, benefits, and value of this national policy, we need national, systematic evaluation and research, similar to that undertaken in California. Monitoring progress is a difficult and complex exercise that involves asking the right questions to obtain relevant answers. One underlying issue is how mitigation planning has better informed and improved federally funded mitigation projects, as well as how such projects have added to the overall resilience of communities. Both questions need further evaluation. In addition, we must ask how mitigation planning has informed and improved local decision making on land-use policy.

There is much value in learning from the experience of individual state efforts to address specific hazards issues and mitigation approaches through specialized general-plan elements or hazard-specific legislation. Mitigation planning under DMA can be additionally enhanced through further examination by FEMA of the value of specialized state requirements. We need more systematic methods to reinforce feedback loops between states and with FEMA. The ongoing meetings of state hazard mitigation officers (SHMOs) are a venue for potentially strengthening these feedback loops.

The connection between mitigation and recovery planning can be strengthened as well. Much valuable recovery experience has evolved from some of the larger disasters in recent years. This should serve as a filter for identifying principles and practices that can further inform mitigation strategies and priorities through identifying recovery-critical facilities essential for continuity of government and essential business. Ultimately, mitigation and recovery planning should go hand in hand.

WHICH ELEMENTS MATTER?

There is no pat set of answers to the question of which elements in a comprehensive plan should address which hazards with what types of linkages to a hazards element, if the plan contains one. While certain answers are relatively straightforward and predictable, others depend on the unique context and circumstances of the community preparing the plan. As a result, most of this section consists of general guidance that, like most models in planning, must be adapted to particular circumstances. There is no substitute for customizing solutions to the specific needs of the jurisdiction for which a plan is being prepared.

Some aspects of hazard mitigation stem from specific state requirements, as noted above. It is more common in states with planning mandates to find significant state guidance accompanying them, but even without mandates many communities might welcome detailed state guidance on planning for hazards of the sort that has characterized recent efforts in Florida and Oregon.

Oregon's Department of Land Conservation and Development (DLCD), which is charged with overseeing the state's growth management program, has produced a series of technical resource guides on planning for specific hazards, such as floods, wildfires, and tsunamis. DLCD currently maintains a natural hazards website that serves the same purpose (www.oregon.gov/LCD/HAZ/about_us.shtml).

The Florida Department of Community Affairs has produced substantial guidance documents on mitigation planning for both wildfires (Florida DCA and Florida DACS 2004) and flooding and coastal storms (Florida DCA 2006), as well as for historic properties (Florida Department of State, Florida DCA, and 1000 Friends of Florida 2006) (all available at www.dca.state.fl.us/fdcp/DCP/publications). The last document is particularly useful in detailing the relationships of various comprehensive plan elements within the Florida growth management system, which requires coastal management elements for jurisdictions in coastal counties, to hazard mitigation priorities within the plan. Because there are few other state documents of comparable thoroughness, it bears examination as a template, though it is essential to keep in mind that other states have both different planning enabling legislation with varying specifications for required or suggested elements in local comprehensive plans and different hazard profiles. In fact, community hazard profiles can often vary significantly even within a state, which can contain both highly vulnerable coastal lowlands and highlands subject to landslides and flooding.

As noted, the central element for coastal hazards analysis in local comprehensive plans in Florida is the coastal management element, which is required specifically for all cities and counties that border the coast. Inland cities and counties, while exempt from that mandate, are statutorily encouraged to develop hazard mitigation and postdisaster redevelopment plans. Florida DCA's guidance also specifically highlights particular elements that should address relevant aspects of natural, especially coastal and flooding, hazards.

Future land use. The future land-use map (FLUM) must coordinate with coastal management strategies to determine appropriate coastal planning area densities. These densities must relate to the "applicable hurricane evacuation plan." Florida also requires coastal communities to include a policy in their comprehensive plans to direct populations away from "coastal high hazard areas"—that is, areas that would be flooded by storm surge from a Category 1 hurricane. While evacuation planning may not always pertain as readily to hazards in noncoastal areas, the use of the future land-use map in identifying potential problems stemming from various densities of development in hazardous areas, such as floodplains, is clear. (See the case study of Charlotte/Mecklenburg County, North Carolina, in Chapter 7.)

Conservation. Increasingly, communities are recognizing the protective features of wetlands, estuarine marshes, and floodplains, which should be identified in the conservation element, along with strategies for protecting and enhancing those features. Regulations in Florida require such identification. Conversely, the coastal management element must include objectives dealing with protection, conservation, or enhancement of coastal wetlands, beaches, and dunes, as well as restoration of beaches and dunes. This effectively links both elements in common purpose.

This particular model is of potential use almost anywhere in the United States; the main variation would involve the specific natural features involved. For instance, protecting wildlife migration corridors along rivers and streams not only serves habitat and environmental protection but also limits development in flood-prone areas. Preserving natural vegetation and woodlands on steep slopes may also serve to reduce the likelihood of dangerous landslides, and conserving natural woodlands without development

ECOLOGY AND MITIGATION

Environmental planning and hazard mitigation are particularly promising areas for cross-fertilization within the comprehensive plan. Natural systems can play a major role in mitigating hazards. Planners must learn enough about that interaction to be able to make informed judgments about the likely results of their decisions in either degrading or enhancing the ability of the natural environment to perform beneficial functions for the built environment. Economists have come to refer to these functions as "ecosystem services." One cannot value those services without knowing what they are. For example, Pilkey et al. (1980, 1998) and the National Research Council (1990), among others, have documented repeatedly the critical role of dune systems and beach vegetation in buffering coastal areas from hurricanes, as well as their inherent instability when disturbed by development. Protecting such natural systems is a first line of defense in protecting our communities.

To explore the ways in which ecological and mitigation concerns could each strengthen the other in the planning process, APA's Hazards Planning Research Center invited several experts to participate in a discussion of this issue. Those involved were:

- Kimberley Bitters, Environmental Specialist, Floodplain Management Program, Ohio Department of Natural Resources

- David Carlton, Engineer, ESA Adolfson

- Craig Colten, Carol O. Sauer Professor, Department of Geography and Anthropology, Louisiana State University

- David Fowler, Milwaukee Metropolitan Sanitation District

- Michele Steinberg, AICP, Firewise Communities Support Manager, National Fire Protection Association

One of the most critical points was raised by Steinberg: In many cases, we are no longer at a point where we can leave nature alone and all will be well. Some environmentalists, notably McKibben (1989), have long decried the imminent reality that no place on earth is untouched by human influences, a situation virtually guaranteed by the prospect of human-induced climate change. For local planners, the point is not to bemoan this condition—because they are by definition working in the built environment—but to determine how to improve both environmental quality and the quality of human life, while also addressing the needs for economic growth and stability.

In the case of floods, we often plan as if stormwater management and hazard mitigation were two separate problems—one of water quality, the other of managing flood risks—but they are inextricably intertwined. Not only is the volume of stormwater influenced by the way we develop watersheds and how we channel runoff to filter pollutants, but floodwaters themselves greatly affect water quality because they pick up everything in their path and deposit much of it downstream. Everyone who has fought floods knows there is nothing clean about floodwaters.

Connecting those ideas creates abundant opportunities for improving the urban environment (see, e.g., Schwab, ed. 2009).

With wildfires, the need for active management has become even clearer and more overwhelming than with floods. As noted in Schwab and Meck (2005), we no longer enjoy the luxury of assuming that forests can be left untended. A history dating to 1910, extensively documented by Pyne (1997), of federal intervention in suppressing forest fires has unintentionally resulted in vastly increased density of biomass, much of it in the form of understory growth that helps spread and exacerbate the intensity of fires at ground level. The problem has been compounded by the widespread late 20th-century introduction of housing and other development into the wildland-urban interface; these structures can rapidly increase the intensity of wildfires, as they typically contain several times the density of combustible materials as the surrounding forests (Rehm et al. 2002).

Effective wildfire mitigation thus virtually demands planning, such as the Community Wildfire Protection Plans (CWPP) resulting from the Healthy Forests Restoration Act of 2003. Our failure or inability to leave the forest alone in the past means we cannot afford to leave it alone now but must manage it with the wisdom of both planning and environmental science.

Steinberg adds that planners need not always "push hazard mitigation as a primary goal" but instead can join the bandwagon if working for a community that is "into sustainability and green," translating those ideas in ways that will aid mitigation in the bargain. Some places, for example, are mitigating floods by allowing streams to flow naturally. The city of Davenport, Iowa, has for years opted to forgo floodwalls along the Mississippi River, instead dedicating green space that can absorb much of the flood (Malin 2009). In forested areas, a community can reintroduce fire through prescribed burning to attain the healthy balance in a fire-adapted ecosystem that is often impeded by the need to suppress fires near housing developments. This, Steinberg says, may even inspire some neighboring communities to better manage their own forests.

Kimberley Bitters expanded on that theme with ideas that form the core of multiple-objective management—the practice of trying to satisfy various public policy objectives through a single program. She cited the "No Adverse Impact" campaign of the Association of State Floodplain Managers (ASFPM). Further, she noted that communities can use the basic requirements of the NFIP as the basis for a framework for flood management in the zoning code but also go beyond the "have-tos" to consider what is best for the community. This may include a range of ecological goods, such as greenways, which create a combination of high-value open space and wildlife habitat that adds value to a community in a number of often intangible ways. Similarly, solutions can address concerns about physical health in a community. For example, the Boulder Creek floodplain in Boulder, Colorado, now hosts an extensive network of trails, which see a high level of bicycle ridership. Bitters proposed that state hazard mitigation teams, in evaluating local projects for funding, use criteria that give priority ratings to projects that include ecological integrity.

(continued on page 35)

may reduce the exposure of the built environment to wildfires. However, few of these measures involve simple answers. Part of the purpose of preparing a conservation element is to assemble the available evidence and research to determine what is known and, more important, what is known to work in combining conservation with risk reduction and other goals for a community. The problems and solutions will vary considerably from one community to another, based on local topography, climate, and natural history. For technical expertise, it is important to know what scientific resources are available to help answer those questions.

Public facilities and services. Protecting natural drainage systems during development is a key starting point for this element. Florida requires that this element contain policies for regulating land use and development that protect these features. It also requires a policy in the coastal element and the capital facilities element that limits public expenditures for infrastructure and public facilities that subsidize development within coastal high-hazard areas (§9J-5.012(3)(b) and §9J-5.016(3)(b)2, F.A.C.). Capital facilities policies are thus used to steer development away from hazardous areas—a strategy that can apply to other types of natural hazards as well.

Closely related issues in public facilities with potential links to hazard mitigation involve goals, objectives, and policies for protecting water treatment facilities, stormwater management, and sewerage and solid waste. In the last case, good predisaster planning might include developing a policy for identifying appropriate staging and storage locations for the extraordinary quantities of debris that often must be disposed of after a disaster.

It is not difficult to imagine other hazard-related linkages in a public facilities element. For example, strict policies for locating facilities for public safety—such as police and fire stations and emergency operations centers—can ensure that these are in safe locations that will not be likely to be affected by hazards. As a matter of public policy, government ought to set a good example for hazard mitigation in the location of any major public facilities, including city halls, libraries, schools, and community centers. To the extent that some of these may double as emergency shelters, the rationale for including safety in siting considerations becomes even stronger.

Transportation. Breakdowns in community transportation systems during disasters are often dramatic and create major dislocations. Examples include the damage to the highway bridges over Lake Pontchartrain from Hurricane Katrina and Florida's Escambia Bay during Hurricane Ivan, as well as the collapse of the Cypress Viaduct during the Loma Prieta earthquake. They make links between transportation planning and hazard mitigation planning essential.

In Florida, the primary link from a transportation element to hazards involves analyzing levels of service for such facilities to determine their adequacy in the event of an evacuation of coastal populations ahead of an oncoming storm. This takes on special significance for barrier-island communities, such as Miami Beach or Sanibel Island, or highly extended and more remote communities, such as the Florida Keys. Yet many mainland communities also face highly constricted transportation corridors under evacuation conditions, particularly those in which the Everglades cut off any westward route. Moreover, some attention must be paid to the evacuation transportation needs of special-needs populations, such as the elderly and disabled. (See the case study of Lee County in Chapter 7.)

Transportation (covered in California and some other places by a *circulation* element) can take on other kinds of significance under other circumstances, many of which may not be under a community's control but which nonetheless can severely affect the community's welfare, safety, and economic activity. One such example is the I-35W bridge collapse (Figure 3.4) in

(continued from page 34)

Craig Colten, who has spent many years studying the evolution of environmental geography in southern Louisiana, said we have done a "poor job of educating people" and a "poor job of maintaining continuity from generation to generation." People still base their reactions to disaster on personal life experiences, he says, while we need to "codify resilience and instill it into education at the ground level." But resilience is an intensely localized quality, so we "need to draw upon local knowledge and adapt plans to local situations. We can't have a rigid checklist."

Optimizing integration of environmental quality and hazard mitigation faces some serious political and institutional obstacles, often when there is a gap between those goals and the forces driving economic development. This could well be planning's greatest challenge in the 21st century. ◄

Figure 3.4. *The Interstate 35W bridge in Minneapolis, shortly after its 2007 collapse*

Minneapolis, which cost lives and forced major reroutings of traffic across the Mississippi River but was the responsibility of the state Department of Transportation. Such potential infrastructure disasters are endemic nationwide. The Minnesota example involved structural failure due to flaws in design, construction, and maintenance without the intervention of natural hazards, but weak infrastructure is more likely to fail in the face of such hazards. Many disasters involve normally sound systems that are pushed beyond their structural limits in unusual or record-setting events, such as the Cedar Rapids and Iowa City (CRANDIC) Railroad bridge collapse in downtown Cedar Rapids, Iowa, during the flood in June 2008. The main goal in such cases may be largely to plan for such contingencies with the best possible workarounds. For transportation facilities directly under community control, on the other hand, more specific planning can be done to attempt to rectify known deficiencies or potential weaknesses. Transportation projects are probably among the most likely to involve direct connections with capital improvements planning and to determine the location and density of patterns of future growth.

Capital improvements. In many states, five-year capital improvement plans are separate from comprehensive plans. Such plans and capital improvements elements alike typically assess costs of desired projects, set priorities, and anticipate future needs based on projected development patterns, which involve links with the future land-use element and, as in the case of Florida, the coastal management element. This element affords a community an opportunity to determine appropriate means of funding the improvements and an annually updated five-year schedule for meeting those needs. Hazard mitigation projects identified in a local hazard mitigation plan ought to be included in a capital improvements plan or element. Florida mandates that communities "include a policy in their *capital improvements element* that includes the elimination of public hazards as a criterion for evaluating local capital improvement projects" (Florida DCA 2006).

Other elements. The list of elements that the Florida DCA recommends includes goals, objectives, and policies related to hazard mitigation. This list is an instructive starting point, but it need not exclude other options. In the end, which elements matter for consideration of hazard-related policies will depend on several factors, among them:

• What elements are mandated or suggested by state planning enabling law and what issues state law says they must or should address

- What hazards have been identified and their specific implications for particular elements of the local comprehensive plan

- What unique opportunities the community may identify for achieving progress on hazard mitigation, particularly when combined with other objectives, such as environmental protection or parks and open space.

Chapter 5 outlines an implementation tool we are calling the *safe growth audit*. It is intended as a thorough means of reviewing local plans, codes, and procedures to determine the best opportunities for advancing hazard mitigation goals. However, checklists can limit the imagination. Planners should help inspire their decision makers and citizens to be more imaginative in identifying opportunities to create a safer, more resilient community. With the focus on civic creativity, here is a short list of other frequently used comprehensive plan elements that could potentially advance hazard mitigation goals:

- *Housing*. Much public and publicly subsidized affordable housing is particularly vulnerable to some natural hazards. In some cases, this is a question of building quality, but it can also be a matter of poor locational choice. The plan can consider how that housing can be retrofitted or replaced to reduce danger to inhabitants in the face of disaster. Mobile homes have posed particular problems of vulnerability, especially in the face of high winds. This element can also address issues of how housing demand is influenced by the desire for siting near natural amenities, which can produce problematic attractions to hazardous locations; the acquisition of older housing stock in riverine floodplains, which may entail replacing some low-cost housing; and the replacement or retrofitting of affordable housing elsewhere in the community. An example of the last might involve seismic retrofitting of older housing built of unreinforced masonry in an area subject to earthquakes.

- *Historic preservation*. Consider the plight of New Orleans in trying to save historic properties, particularly in view of their role in attracting tourism. Florida has an informative, detailed guidebook on protecting historic resources (Florida Department of State, Florida DCA, and 1000 Friends of Florida 2006), but such guides can be found elsewhere in the country, including some specific to floods or earthquakes.

- *Economic development*. Specific local policies regarding issues of crucial importance to business continuity can aid economic recovery, while technical assistance in support of hazard mitigation for vulnerable small businesses may keep some afloat in the face of disaster. One such example might involve undergrounding utilities in a business district, which can often be accomplished through special assessments, tax increment financing, or similar devices limited to the area of the improvement. Moreover, a safe community is inherently a place where it makes sense to locate a business. Economic development officials in Roseville, California (see case study in Chapter 7) have learned the advantages of marketing the city's safety to potential new businesses. In the case of Bourne, Massachusetts, which has no other location options for the central business district, flood hazard mitigation became an absolute necessity in the eyes of the business community. (See Chapter 8.)

- *Recreation and open space*. Turning vulnerable floodplain land into open space or recreational areas can help avert or minimize disaster by sacrificing park land in the short term instead of allowing floodwaters to ruin homes and businesses. Land acquisition choices for open space can be guided at least in part by hazard mitigation objectives, as often found in communities that seek to protect and provide public access to areas that are also deemed potentially hazardous for development, such as riverfronts and beaches.

- *Environment/natural resources*. Though akin to considerations described above for a Florida conservation element, this element could be used to go much further. For instance, wise decisions about land use and building design might mitigate a combination of natural hazards and industrial development that could otherwise exacerbate losses and the contamination of floodwater. Although the 1993 Midwest floods reportedly put 59 U.S. Environmental Protection Agency National Priority List (Superfund) sites underwater (Galloway 1995)—to say nothing of brownfield sites, gasoline stations, and leaky underground storage tanks—better land-use planning might have averted some of those collisions of natural forces and hazardous materials. Closely related to an environmental element would be a critical and sensitive areas element, used by some jurisdictions to focus on planning for a specific area that has unusually high priority for protection of natural features or resources. These are sometimes done as separate plans (see Chapter 5).

- *Implementation*. Many comprehensive plans contain an implementation element that discusses how the plan's goals, objectives, and policies will be achieved and over what time frames. While specific projects requiring capital investment by the local jurisdiction should appear in the capital improvements program or element, implementation can include other policies and programs that do not require such investment or are contingent on outside funding sources, although they may involve budgetary commitments for personnel, enforcement, consultant fees, or other outlays. Revising a zoning or other land-use code to conform to a new plan is one particularly common activity in this regard, and the major commitment to achieving this objective typically involves budgeting staff time for it. While many hazard mitigation objectives might be subsumed under such larger agendas, it is important that they at least be identified as part of those implementation objectives.

SHOULD THERE BE A HAZARDS ELEMENT?

In some states, communities are required by state law to prepare some type of hazards element in their comprehensive plans. In most states, the issue is a matter of choice, as is the decision to prepare a plan at all. In states where there is no required hazards element, a local hazard mitigation plan may be developed separately from the comprehensive plan solely as an exercise to meet federal requirements. In states where the comprehensive plan has the effect of law, the only way to give the priorities of the local hazard mitigation plan such meaning and effectiveness is to integrate those priorities directly or by reference into the comprehensive plan.

Creating a hazards element in a comprehensive plan can be seen as a superfluous exercise in view of the effort already going into a local hazard mitigation plan. Why should a community do the same work twice? However, the work need not be duplicative. A hazards element can incorporate all or most of the content or findings of a hazard mitigation plan by reference, and ideally the two documents would differ little, if at all, in overall content. However, to achieve effective interoperability between the two documents, it is essential that the planners involved prepare both with an eye to what is needed for federal approval of the local hazard mitigation plan. This would be consistent with the recommendations of Boswell et al. (2008) to the California Governor's Office of Emergency Services (OES)—that "local jurisdictions

TABLE 3.2. POTENTIAL RELEVANCE OF DISASTER TYPES TO MITIGATION PROVISIONS IN COMPREHENSIVE PLAN ELEMENTS

Type of Plan Element	Flood	Coastal Hazards (includes tsunami)	Seismic	Wildfire	Tornado	Landslide	Volcano
Hazards	x	x	x	x	x	x	x
Land Use	x	x					
Conservation	x	x		x		x	x
Public Facilities	x	x	x	x	x	x	x
Transport	x	x	x	x		x	x
Capital Improvements	x	x	x	x	x	x	x
Housing	x	x	x	x	x	x	
Historic Preservation	x	x	x	x		x	
Economic Development	x	x	x	x		x	
Recreation and Open Space	x	x	x (near fault lines)	x		x	x
Environment	x	x	x	x		x	x
Implementation	x	x	x	x	x	x	x

Source: James C. Schwab

should be encouraged to take advantage of the financial benefits of AB 2140 by either creating integrated LHMP-Safety Elements or by adopting their LHMP as an annex to their Safety Element." As an implementation strategy, the same report noted that "updating the Safety Element at the same time of LHMP preparation would maximize work and be an efficient process." It also recommended that OES "conduct outreach, education, and technical assistance programs" for such integration, a step that many other state hazard mitigation officers (SHMOs) and emergency management agencies could also undertake. However, the challenge in many states would be providing SHMOs an adequate understanding of comprehensive planning in order to be able to undertake such an effort.

Most states currently have a long way to go in achieving the kinds of plan and policy integration envisioned in Boswell's study, and even California has work ahead to reach the same goal. There may also be resistance in some quarters to moving in this direction because of bureaucratic turf issues and political resistance to new mandates. Nonetheless, doing so makes sense as a matter of efficiency and effective implementation. Florida has provided some clear guidelines in this respect. (See Florida DCA 2006, Secs, 3.1, 4.1, 4.2, and 4.3.)

LINKING PLAN ELEMENTS

If it makes sense to integrate hazard mitigation into the local comprehensive plan, both through a hazards element (whatever it may be called) and through specific provisions in other elements, then it makes sense to establish clear linkages among policies in those elements. In plans that are online, hyperlinking those cross-references aids the user in understanding the integration of hazard mitigation efforts. It also makes clear to the public and to local government agencies who is working with whom to achieve what objectives.

Effective linkage can be achieved by any jurisdiction that is thinking holistically in the development of its comprehensive plan, as demonstrated in Morgan County, Utah. (See Chapter 8.) This largely rural, sparsely populated jurisdiction is predominantly interested in maintaining its bucolic quality of life. While many rural areas tend to assume that keeping things as they are means avoiding planning, Morgan County uses planning as a tool for preserving its rural values. As a result, natural hazards are addressed in goals throughout the plan, in elements including Community Character, Land Use, and Environment. Protecting fragile areas from development is a mitigation goal that is also a quality-of-life and environmental quality goal. Hazard mitigation is driven at least in part by an even larger community vision, and the integration and linkages within the plan come naturally as a result.

While the Morgan County example may seem more organic in nature, there are models and tools for achieving effective linkages very deliberately. The *Growing Smart Legislative Guidebook* (Meck 2002) produced by APA includes model state enabling requirements for a Natural Hazards Element. (See www .planning.org/growingsmart, Section 7-210.) It is not difficult to translate such state planning language into a model for constructing effective cross-element linkages between a hazards element and other elements of a local comprehensive plan. The driving force, however, will inevitably be the local political will to make hazard mitigation a planning priority.

NOTE

1. The Association of Bay Area Governments describes soft-story buildings thus: "Many apartments and condos can collapse in earthquakes because they have parking, 'tuck-under' parking, or open commercial space on the first floor, making this story 'weak' or 'soft' and likely to lean or even fall over in earthquakes." See http://quake.abag.ca.gov/mitigation/PR-Soft-Story-11-17.pdf.

CHAPTER 4

Integrating Hazard Mitigation into Other Local Plans

James C. Schwab, AICP

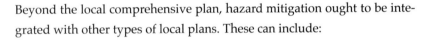

Beyond the local comprehensive plan, hazard mitigation ought to be integrated with other types of local plans. These can include:

- Area plans—also known as subarea, small area, or sector plans—which focus on specific parts of a community, including the central business district, particular neighborhoods, or traffic corridors;

- Functional plans, which focus on particular community services or functions, such as sewer and water, transit, park development, or stormwater management; and

- Operational plans, such as emergency operations or continuity of operations for government agencies (also known as continuity-of-government plans).

Even though not all communities have comprehensive plans, nearly all will have some other types of plans in place, often including hazard mitigation plans. The implementation rules for the DMA amendments to the Stafford Act in the Code of Federal Regulations establish the federal intent that local governments integrate those plans. The clearest statement on this point is in Section 201.6(c)(4)(ii), which states that mitigation plan content "shall include":

> (4) A plan maintenance process that includes:

> (ii) A process by which local governments incorporate the requirements of the mitigation plan into other planning mechanisms such as comprehensive or capital improvement plans, when appropriate.

This point is reinforced in the FEMA "Blue Book":

> Jurisdictions **shall** indicate how mitigation recommendations will be incorporated into comprehensive plans, capital improvement plans, zoning and building codes, site reviews, permitting, job descriptions, staff training, and other planning tools, where such tools are the appropriate vehicles for implementation.

> Communities that do not have a comprehensive plan, or other similar planning mechanisms, *should* explain how the mitigation recommendations would be implemented. Further, for certain mitigation actions that may use other means of implementation, these other tools should be described. (FEMA 2009, 3.47)

In short, whatever planning mechanisms a community may have available to use in implementing its mitigation plan recommendations, it is expected to use them and detail their planned use in the local mitigation plan. As a matter of sound practice, many jurisdictions inventory and review other local plans in developing a local hazard mitigation plan, not only as a way of meeting the FEMA requirements but to identify gaps, weaknesses, or opportunities for enhancing plan integration.

AREA PLANS

Area plans are meant to address issues unique or specific to parts of a jurisdiction. These subareas may be defined in a number of ways for various purposes, all largely dependent on the planning objectives of the community. Cities often delineate planning boundaries for individual neighborhoods, and a few (such as Dayton, Ohio, and New York City) have created neighborhood planning councils that have the authority to review plans, zoning changes, and other development issues and to make recommendations to the citywide planning commission. After Hurricane Katrina, for example, New Orleans undertook what became the Unified New Orleans Plan, which contains a series of neighborhood plans for the city's officially delineated planning districts (UNOP 2007). The new draft master plan under consideration in the fall of 2009 also proposed expanding the city planning staff to include a team of neighborhood planners to strengthen the role of neighborhood planning (New Orleans 2009). Some neighborhood plans may have the specific intent of addressing historic preservation needs or the conservation of existing neighborhood character. Other types of area plans, however, may focus on business districts, such as a downtown or central business district or a commercial corridor.

As with any part of a community, subareas will face issues involving natural or other hazards that can be addressed more effectively and in greater detail in an area plan than may be possible in a community-wide comprehensive plan. In some cases, these still may be issues that demand community-wide or even broader attention. The issue of levee repairs and land use in adjoining districts in various parts of New Orleans is an obvious example, as it involves the collaboration of the levee district, the city, and the U.S. Army Corps of Engineers, as well as other institutions and special districts at times. All plans at all levels of government can raise issues that cannot be resolved without extensive intergovernmental or even international cooperation. An area plan should give those area-specific issues the attention they deserve, and it should provide residents, property owners, and other stakeholders the opportunity to provide input in decisions that may affect them. It also affords the opportunity to vet strategies for marshaling the needed resources and funds to get a specific task accomplished. Examples might include plan proposals for special assessment districts or business improvement districts or appeals to the private sector to help underwrite specific programs or improvements.

Concern for the long-term survival of a business district in an area prone to flooding, coastal storms, or earthquakes can be the driving force behind hazard mitigation in downtown and corridor plans. The case study of Bourne, Massachusetts (Chapter 8), delves into the predicament that drove a downtown business group to underwrite a report on flood-hazard mitigation for the Main Street Business District in order to address unavoidable coastal-flooding hazards.

The use of area plans is not limited to urban locations, as seen in the case study of Morgan County, Utah (Chapter 8). This highly rural and mountainous county's comprehensive plan includes eight area plans written by residents to deal with specific problems. One area, Mountain Green, pushed the county to pay more attention to hazards as the result of a slow-moving landslide that eventually damaged several homes. The case of Morgan County also illustrates ways in which issues of environmental quality can blend with hazard mitigation in a rural county and within the subareas of such a jurisdiction.

Environmental considerations can themselves form the basis for an area plan. Often, such a plan may have serious hazard mitigation implications, even if they are not the plan's primary focus. Critical- and sensitive-area plans, whether independent plans or elements of comprehensive plans, provide "a framework for identifying the resources, determining what will be protected, and identifying mechanisms for protecting them" (Witten 2006). The protection of critical environmental resources often serves a mitigation purpose that should be recognized in both the hazard mitigation plan and the critical- and sensitive-areas plan. One example is the storm-buffering impact of coastal wetlands, the gradual loss of which is a major and growing concern in New Orleans and other southern Louisiana communities. Other examples might include the protection of steep slopes from erosion that could in turn produce both landslides and increased downstream flooding.

FUNCTIONAL PLANS

Functional plans, which are often prepared at a regional level but can also be local, address specific planning topics such as parks and open space, bike access, water quality and supply, sewage and solid waste management, transportation, cultural amenities, and more. They are stand-alone plans that focus on specific public services and functions.

Such plans are often produced by special districts and independent agencies that are outside the direct administrative authority of local officials. As a result, appropriately integrating hazard mitigation priorities into these plans requires intergovernmental coordination between, for example, cities and water management districts, stormwater utilities, or public-utility districts. Planners and emergency managers who want to see specific hazard mitigation concerns addressed in these plans often need to cultivate ongoing discussions and relationships with agency decision makers and planners. Ideally, this leads to the regular exchange of information for mutual planning purposes.

One area in which the need for coordination is especially evident is flood control and floodplain management. The protection of drinking water supplies for large metropolitan areas often also involves coordination with state or federal agencies responsible for critical protective infrastructure, such as dams and levee systems, which may well have special plans of their own. Moreover, catastrophic failure of such systems can have profound impacts on large populations, as the 1993 flooding and forced shutdown of the water treatment plant in Des Moines, Iowa, demonstrated (Schwab et al., 1998, chap. 1).

The case study of Charlotte/Mecklenburg County, North Carolina (Chapter 7), stands out as one that illustrates multiple levels of coordination among a variety of special plans and guidelines for such functions as greenways, stormwater, and water supply. That region has also prepared watershed-based flood mitigation plans for use across the county. Water management and flood control issues in the region are particularly complex. In addition to hazard mitigation they entail consideration of upland forest retention and watershed management as means of controlling regional growth and limiting stormwater runoff. This in turn entails interactions with the regional electric utility's hydropower development and with stormwater management plans for specific watersheds (Kollin 2009).

The roles of various functional plans can contribute to the complexity of hazard mitigation, but that makes integration of hazard mitigation priorities all the more important. The large and growing array of approved local hazard mitigation plans includes numerous special districts that have undertaken such plans in order to comply with DMA and become eligible for federal mitigation grants.

OPERATIONAL PLANS

Operational plans generally deal with the management and coordination of certain functions of local or regional government. The two types most relevant to planners dealing with hazard mitigation are emergency operations plans, which are most commonly the responsibility of emergency managers, and continuity-of-operations plans, which lay out how a particular entity plans to maintain its functionality in the event of an emergency. This latter type of plan is particularly important for any type of critical facility.

An emergency operations plan "predetermines actions to be taken by government agencies and private organizations in response to an emergency or disaster event" (Schwab, Eschelbach, and Brower 2007). Keeping these plans current requires running drills and drawing lessons from exercises with risk scenarios. For more than a decade, FEMA has provided local governments with postdisaster exercises involving floods, earthquakes, and hurricanes. Although most local emergency-operations plans do not address hazard mitigation, opportunities to do so in the context of predisaster preparedness and postdisaster response and recovery can arise; there is no reason for such plans to conflict. At the very least, emergency managers and planners should collaborate to ensure that there are opportunities to address hazard mitigation in a postdisaster setting, since they both aim to reduce losses and protect lives and property.

One salient example of the need for extensive coordination among government agencies is the potential for levee failures in the Sacramento–San Joaquin Delta in California. The Delta Emergency Operations Plan (California

Department of Water Resources 2007) includes extensive risk assessments of the possibility of multiple levee failures, a truly alarming scenario that should provoke the incorporation of recommended mitigation actions into state and local mitigation plans. The work supporting the emergency operations plan can then support the risk assessment and proposed actions in the mitigation plan, though such integration can also work in the opposite direction (Figure 4.1).

Risk assessments have also been listed as one of eight sound practices for continuity-of-operations planning (U.S. GAO 2005). This, too, offers a possible point of integration with hazard mitigation plans. In reviewing the continuity planning of federal agencies, the U.S. Government Accountability Office reviewed the published literature and consulted experts to develop its list, which included:

Michael Nevins, U.S. Army Corps of Engineers

Figure 4.1. *Aerial view of a broken levee and the resultant flooding on the Sacramento River in the Sacramento River delta*

Perform a risk and impact analysis for each essential function—including prioritization of essential functions and determination of minimum acceptance level of output and recovery time objective for each function.

Continuity-of-operations planning in the public sector has a direct parallel with contingency planning, widely used in the private sector and also known as business continuity planning. Regardless of the name, the underlying purpose is to develop "advance arrangements and procedures that enable an organization to respond to a disaster so that critical business functions resume within a defined time frame, the amount of loss is minimized, and the stricken facilities are repaired or replaced as soon as possible" (Schwab, Eschelbach, and Brower 2007). Critical public facilities most significantly include water treatment plants, sewage treatment plants, hospitals, and public safety facilities. The frequent, necessary proximity of water-related facilities to floodplains makes preparation for flood emergencies especially important. For instance, plans for maintaining water treatment and distribution were critical to public safety and survival in Cedar Rapids, Iowa, during the June 2008 floods that overwhelmed the city's downtown. Such system failures can have massive cascading consequences, including the inability to fight fires. According to Schwab, Eschelbach, and Brower (2007), a comprehensive approach consists of three main elements: property protection, contingency planning, and insurance.

While planners often will not be directly involved in developing or executing such plans, they should be aware of such plans, what they contain, and how they may affect the community's hazard mitigation strategies, particularly but not exclusively as they pertain to protection of critical facilities. As with emergency operations plans, coordination and communication among planners, public safety professionals, and emergency managers are important. FEMA (2007) delineated coordination as one of eight "principles of emergency management" in a document promulgated through its Emergency Management Institute. It emphasized the necessity of "big picture" thinking and noted that emergency managers "are seldom in a position to direct the activities of the many agencies and organizations involved." This is the very position in which planners most often find themselves as they seek to coordinate numerous local government priorities. Both planners and emergency managers must know how to coordinate within their respective realms in order to be effective because neither group can do it all itself. Moreover, FEMA stated that it "requires that the emergency manager gain agreement among these disparate agencies as to common purpose and then ensure that their independent activities help to achieve this common purpose." In other words, both planners and emergency managers are more likely to be successful if they are skilled at building consensus. Both professions have a major stake in finding common ground in establishing goals for hazard mitigation through integrated planning.

FEMA (2007) differentiates between coordination and collaboration, noting that "current usage often makes it difficult to distinguish between these words." But it adds that coordination "refers to a process designed to ensure that functions, roles, and responsibilities are identified and tasks accomplished; collaboration must be viewed as an attitude or an organizational culture that characterizes the degree of unity and cooperation that exists within a community. In essence, collaboration creates the environment in which coordination can function effectively."

CHAPTER 5

Integrating Hazards into the Implementation Tools of Planning

David R. Godschalk, FAICP

 What is the aim of integrating hazards into planning implementation tools? In answering this question, consider the significant hazard mitigation goals that can be pursued in the course of planning implementation. Knowledge of the desired goals can suggest the type of implementation tool or combination of tools that can achieve them.

This chapter focuses on the primary planning implementation tools under the purview of local planners—zoning, subdivision regulations, and capital improvement programs—although it recognizes that tools designed by other agencies, such as building codes, and public outreach programs also play important roles in implementation.[1]

GOALS OF INTEGRATING HAZARDS INTO PLANNING IMPLEMENTATION TOOLS

Integrating hazards into planning implementation tools has three primary goals:

- *Keeping future development out of known hazard areas.* The purpose here is to influence the *location* of public and private investment, guiding it away from known hazard areas and toward safe growth locations. For example, zoning and subdivision regulations can direct private development away from hazard areas through designation of location-specific allowable land uses and standards for public safety. Capital improvement programs (CIPs) can direct funding for public facilities such as roads, bridges, utility systems, and critical facilities to locations outside hazard areas.

- *Keeping hazards from affecting existing developed areas.* The purpose here is to improve *protection* of already built-up areas through structural mitigation projects or environmental management techniques that modify the progression of the hazard itself, using combinations of local funds from CIPs and funds from state and federal programs. For example, dams and levees can be constructed to provide a certain amount of protection from future flooding for low-lying developed areas, while reforestation and wetland preservation can be used for flood control.

- *Strengthening existing development to resist hazards.* The purpose here is to enhance *hazard resistance* by enacting and enforcing construction code provisions concerning hazard stresses and impacts. For example, hazard area zones and subdivision regulations, as well as building codes, can contain design standards and project review procedures for ensuring the safety of projects subject to earthquake, landslide, wildfire, and flood hazards.

Each planning implementation tool has particular powers appropriate for implementing hazard safety. We next consider where hazard mitigation fits into individual tools—*zoning, subdivision regulations, capital improvement programs* (see Schwab et al. 1998, chap. 5; Godschalk 2007; and Tobin and Montz 1997)—and then we propose a strategy for analyzing the overall effectiveness of the complete package of local implementation tools: using *safe growth audits.*

WHERE HAZARDS FIT IN THE ZONING CODE

Zoning ordinances are among the planner's most effective tools for limiting damage from hazards. They have the ability to restrict development in hazardous areas to land uses that will not suffer extensive disaster losses, and they can encourage growth in safe locations. They achieve this by specifying the location, type, amount, density, and characteristics of development permitted in mapped zoning districts. Where and how these development characteristics are applied affects both the physical and the social vulnerability of the jurisdiction.

The characteristics of each natural hazard inherent in a jurisdiction determine how ways to address that hazard fit into the jurisdiction's zoning code. For example, floods, the most common hazard for most communities, occur in low-lying areas adjacent to water bodies. The boundaries of these floodplains are established by FEMA on Flood Insurance Rate Maps (FIRMs), along with estimates of how frequently a location can expect to see floods of various depths. If floods are an important local hazard, then designated floodplains must be incorporated into the zoning map and regulations.

Flood zoning typically is implemented through placement of floodplain boundaries on the local zoning map and the use of various regulations to enforce restrictions on development in and adjacent to those floodplains. The most common regulation prohibits development within the most hazardous part of the floodplain—the *floodway* channel where water flows and where obstructions would limit the channel and increase downstream flooding. It also limits the density (or amount of obstruction) that can be placed in the *flood fringe* area, which is within the floodplain but outside the floodway.

Other flood zoning elements include *use regulations* that permit only open-space land uses within floodplains; *setbacks* to minimize flood exposure of buildings and to provide waterfront buffers, maintain natural vegetation, and limit runoff; *nonconforming-use* regulations that prescribe standards for allowable reconstruction of flood-damaged structures; *special-use permits* that require development to meet established criteria or conditions to minimize future flooding; and *overlay districts* that add a separate level of regulation to sensitive hazard areas, such as floodplains. For an example of an ordinance that incorporates all of these elements, see the sidebar on the Chapel Hill Resource Conservation District (p. 50).

Coastal-zone management regulations constitute a special case of flood zoning that may use the same devices but also must contend with shoreline erosion and therefore include provisions, such as setbacks, to deal with ocean dynamics (see Godschalk, Brower, and Beatley 1989). *Hurricane zoning* safeguards against still-water flooding, storm surge, and wind damage. Still-water flooding (A Zones) and coastal flooding with wave action (V Zones) hazard areas are delineated on FIRMs. Specific elevation and building construction standards are applied within A and V zones. Wind-damage zones are identified and protection standards are specified in building codes. Since hurricanes are often accompanied by severe erosion, special setbacks may be required. For example, in North Carolina, minimum ocean setbacks of 60 feet for single-family and two-family residential dwellings and 120 feet for multifamily and commercial buildings are required. Height and bulk regulations are used to reduce density in areas subject to hurricane hazards.

Earthquake and geologic hazards zoning is implemented through mapping of seismic areas and restricting development in and adjacent to them. For example, a California law requires the state geologist to map seismic hazard zones, sellers of real property to disclose the zones' existence, and local jurisdictions to conduct a site-specific investigation for all development proposals in order to ensure acceptable levels of earthquake risk before issuing a development permit.[2]

Earthquakes and associated geologic hazards, such as landslides and debris flows, may be regulated by means of a *natural hazards overlay zone*, such as the one adopted by Utah County. (See sidebar, p. 52). This overlay zone allows the underlying uses from the zoning map but requires that uses and facilities vulnerable to geologic hazards be protected against collapse or severe damage at the time of construction or placement in the zone.

Wildfire zoning is applied in jurisdictions subject to intense, uncontrolled, rapidly spreading fires that sweep through forests or chaparral. The goal of wildfire zoning is to manage conditions in the urban-wildland interface, as well as in other forest or recreation areas with high wildfire potential. Zoning regulations can reduce residential densities or encourage cluster development patterns in the most vulnerable interfaces. Wildfire risk also can be reduced by using nonflammable building materials, planting fire-resistant vegetation, and constructing firebreaks and safety zones around residential areas and public facilities in the urban-wildland interface.

CHAPEL HILL RESOURCE CONSERVATION DISTRICT (EXCERPTS)

The resource conservation district (RCD) is applied to the areas within and along watercourses within the town's planning jurisdiction in order to preserve the water quality of the town's actual or potential water supply sources, to minimize danger to lives and properties from flooding in and near the watercourses, to preserve the water-carrying capacity of the watercourses and to protect them from erosion and sedimentation, to retain open spaces and greenways and to protect their environmentally sensitive character, to preserve urban wildlife and plant life habitats from the intrusions of urbanization, to provide air and noise buffers to ameliorate the effects of development, and to preserve and maintain the aesthetic qualities and appearance of the town.

Permitted uses in the RCD depend on location within the Stream Corridor Zones, which are defined relative to the distance from the stream bank, as shown in the illustration below.

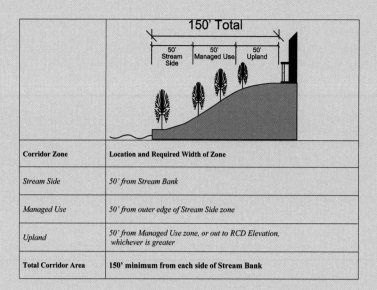

Corridor Zone	Location and Required Width of Zone
Stream Side	50' from Stream Bank
Managed Use	50' from outer edge of Stream Side zone
Upland	50' from Managed Use zone, or out to RCD Elevation, whichever is greater
Total Corridor Area	150' minimum from each side of Stream Bank

PERMITTED USES WITHIN RESOURCE CONSERVATION DISTRICT

(A)	(B)	(C)	(D)
Use	Stream Side Zone	Managed Use Zone	Upland Zone
Trails, greenways, open space, parks, and other similar public recreational uses and private recreational uses that do not require fertilizers, pesticides, or extensive fences, or walls	P	P	P
Outdoor horticulture, forestry, wildlife sanctuary, and similar agricultural and related uses that do not require land-disturbing activities or pesticides, or extensive fences or walls	P	P	P
Pastures or plant nurseries that do not require land-disturbing activities or pesticides, or extensive fences or walls	N	P	P
Gardens, play areas and other similar uses which do not require pesticides for routine maintenance	N	P	P
Lawns, golf course fairways, play fields and other areas which may require fertilizers or pesticides	N	N	P
Archery ranges, picnic structures, playground equipment and other similar public and private recreational uses that do not require fertilizers, pesticides, or extensive fences or walls	N	P	P

(continued on page 51)

(continued from page 50)

PERMITTED USES WITHIN RESOURCE CONSERVATION DISTRICT (*CONTINUED*)

(A)	(B)	(C)	(D)
Use	Stream Side Zone	Managed Use Zone	Upland Zone
Public utility and storm drainage facilities where there is a practical necessity to their location within the RCD	P	P	P
Streets, bridges, and other similar transportation facilities where there is a practical necessity to their location within the RCD	S	S	S
Sidewalks	P	P	P
Accessory land-disturbing activities ordinarily associated with a single-family or two-family dwelling, such as fences, gardens, and similar uses	N	P	P
Driveways and utility service lines when there is a practical necessity	P	P	P
Public maintenance of streets, bridges, other similar transportation facilities and/or public utility and storm drainage facilities	P	P	P
Detention/retention basin and associated infrastructure	N	P	P
Lakes, ponds, and associated infrastructure, such as dams, spillways, riser pipes and stilling basins, that are located outside of the regulatory floodplain, shall be permitted with a Special Use Permit	S	S	S
Stream and riparian area restoration and maintenance	P	P	P

"P" means the activity is permitted as of right, "N" means that the activity is prohibited; "S" means that the activity is permitted only upon approval of a special use permit or a subdivision application by the town council.

The resource conservation district elevation is defined to be the elevation three feet above the 100-year floodplain elevation. The 100-year floodplain elevation shall be established as the regulatory floodplain as delineated in the flood insurance rate maps, flood boundary floodway maps, and Flood Insurance Study for the Town of Chapel Hill, or where the base flood elevations and flood hazard factors have not been determined, the 100-year floodplain plan elevation shall be calculated using engineering methodology compatible with that used to develop the flood insurance rate maps, flood boundary, floodway maps, and flood insurance study.

Standards for development in the resource conservation district include:

- The lowest floor elevation of all permanent structures (buildings) shall be placed at least eighteen (18) inches above the resource conservation district elevation and in such a manner as not to adversely impede the flow of waters.

- Wherever practicable no stormwater discharge shall be allowed directly off an impervious surface into a stream channel.

- Utility lines, roads and driveways shall be located parallel to the flow of waters. Where a road, driveway, or utility line necessarily must cross a watercourse, such crossing shall allow convenient access by wildlife and shall safely convey floodwaters to the same extent as before construction of the crossings.

- The site plan shall minimize adverse environmental and flooding effects. Permanent structures shall be located as far from the watercourse, and as close to the outer boundary of the resource conservation district, as is practical, and shall be clustered as much as practical, to minimize land disturbance, to maximize undeveloped open space, and to maximize retention of natural vegetation and buffers.

- Water supply, sanitary sewer, and on-site waste disposal systems shall be designed to prevent the infiltration of flood waters into the system(s), prevent discharges from the system(s) into flood waters and, avoid impairment during flooding to minimize flood damage.

- Cutting or filling shall be permitted within the watercourse only if the resulting change to the hydraulic characteristics of the watercourse will reduce or maintain the water surface elevation during the base flood discharge in the vicinity of the development; however, in no case will cutting or filling be permitted within the watercourse if greater than a one foot per second increase in the velocity would result; or if greater than one-half (1/2) foot rise in the base flood elevation would result.

Source: http://library1.municode.com/default-test/template.htm?view=browse &doc_action=setdoc&doc_keytype=tocid&doc_key=5d1c1b1b79939075bd0f03 8b721a1e5e&infobase=19952, sec. 3.6.3.

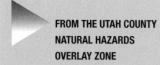

FROM THE UTAH COUNTY NATURAL HAZARDS OVERLAY ZONE

The specific purposes and intent of the County Commission in establishing the NHO Natural Hazards Overlay Zone are:

1. To take advantage of the powers and more fully implement the basic purposes for planning and zoning and to implement the plans.

2. To implement the joint program of the Utah Geologic and Mineral Survey, the U.S. Geological Survey, and Utah County to identify geologic hazards and reduce the risk therefrom.

3. To protect human life and health.

4. To minimize damage to public and private property.

5. To minimize the need for rescue and relief efforts associated with hazards and disasters, which efforts occur at public expense.

6. To minimize the damage to essential public facilities including (but not limited to) water and gas mains; electric, telephone and sewer lines; and roads and bridges.

7. To maintain a stable tax base by providing for the sound use and development of areas affected by geologic hazards so as to minimize post-disaster blight.

8. To assure that those who occupy the areas susceptible to geologic hazards assume responsibility for their actions regarding land use, construction, and grading.

9. To notify owners and buyers of land in the NHO Zone of the potential for rockfall, debris flow, landslide, or surface fault rupture.

In order to accomplish the stated purposes and intent, the provisions of the NHO Zone:

a. Restrict or prohibit those uses which are dangerous to health,

(continued on page 53)

The San Luis Obispo County Land Use Ordinance defines fire hazards based on the type of vegetation (fuel potential) present, as shown in Table 5.1 and mapped in the safety element of the county's general plan.

Transfer of development rights (TDR) is a zoning-based technique that allows property owners in defined *sending* areas to sell their development rights to property owners in *receiving* areas. The sending areas, which may include hazard areas as well as agricultural lands and other areas, are downzoned to a low density. The receiving areas, which are planned to accommodate urban growth, are upzoned to a higher density that is permitted when development rights are applied. For example, Sarasota County, Florida, designates its barrier islands as the sending zone, with the receiving zone located on higher and drier terrain.

Climate change due to greenhouse gas emissions increases risks of drought, sea-level rise, and decreased air quality. Climate scientists have identified two types of responses to climate change: (1) *avoiding* its unmanageable impacts (preparing for climate warming by reducing vulnerability to the impacts) and (2) *managing* the avoidable impacts (slowing climate warming by reducing greenhouse gas emissions). The terminology can be confusing, however, since "mitigation" in the field of emergency management refers to predisaster actions to reduce damage and injury from natural hazards, a definition that includes *both* adaptation and mitigation measures.

Zoning implementation offers a means to *mitigate* climate change effects through policies to guide the location, type, and amount of land-using buildings and activities, as well as the preservation of open space and agricultural lands to minimize or even sequester carbon emissions. It also can aid in *adaptation* to the impacts of climate change, such as sea-level rise, by redirecting future settlement patterns away from existing or anticipated future hazard areas. For an example, see the California climate change bill, SB 375.[3]

Accelerated sea-level rise associated with climate change is leading to increased exposure of people and property to coastal hazards. Adverse consequences include increased vulnerability to losses of lives and property from flooding; increased vulnerability to property losses and losses of recreational areas from accelerated erosion of beaches and dune systems; increased salinity of drinking-water aquifers and of estuaries and wetlands; diminished effectiveness of stormwater drainage systems; and retreat or,

TABLE 5.1. POTENTIAL FOR RANGE, BRUSH, AND FOREST FIRES, BY TYPE OF PLANT COMMUNITY, SAN LUIS OBISPO COUNTY

WILDLAND FIRE HAZARD FUEL POTENTIAL			
Very High	**High**	**Moderate**	
Chaparral	North Coastal Scrub	Riparian Woodland	Beach-Dune
	Foothill Woodland	North Coastal Grassland	Coast Sand Plains
	Juniper/Oak Woodland	Evergreen Forest	Saline Plains
		Interior Herbaceous	Coastal Salt Marsh
		Desert Scrub	Freshwater Marsh

San Luis Obispo 2008

where retreat is not possible, loss of wetlands and the biological communities they support.

Changes in the land's surface features may be at least as important in altering the weather as changes associated with greenhouse gases (Pielke 2005). Conversion of vegetated areas to urban and agricultural uses induces regional temperature and precipitation change. Forests can play a significant role in mitigating such climate change. Deforestation can change the global atmospheric concentration of carbon dioxide, as well as affect the local, regional, and global climate by changing the energy balance on the earth's surface.

WHERE HAZARDS FIT IN THE SUBDIVISION CODE

Subdivision regulations govern the basic processes of dividing land into salable parcels and servicing those lots with roads, water, and sewer systems. Awareness of and sensitivity to hazards are critical in the design and implementation of subdivision regulations because, once individual property rights have been established by sales of lots to individual buyers, it is almost impossible to change the resulting urban form. If a subdivision is allowed to be created in a hazard area, then the die is cast and one more neighborhood will be subjected to an unacceptable level of future hazard risks.

Many jurisdictions combine their zoning and subdivision regulations in a single unified land-use ordinance or unified development ordinance. The unified land-use ordinance of San Luis Obispo County, California, is a good example. Allowable land uses and permit requirements (zoning) are described in one article, while subsequent articles describe site planning and project design standards, subdivision design standards, and transfer of development credits. The ordinance includes specific regulations for flood, wildfire, earthquake, and coastal hazards. (See sidebar, p. 54.)

Subdivision location and design can either reduce or worsen vulnerability to natural hazards. Obviously, location on or adjacent to hazard-prone lands, such as landslide or floodplain areas, heightens the risk of disasters. Placement of roads, residential lots, and public facilities within subdivision projects can clearly increase hazard risks by reducing evacuation or public safety access. Less obviously, increases in impervious surfaces can generate increased stormwater runoff, heightening flooding risks, while failure to conserve natural vegetation and environmental features, such as wetlands and dunes, can reduce the capacity of the environment to contain or absorb hazard forces.

Subdivision regulations can use techniques intended to promote design flexibility—such as cluster development, planned unit development, conservation subdivisions, and density transfer—for hazard mitigation purposes. For example, in a subdivision proposed for a property containing floodplains, the area to be developed can be clustered on the upland portion of the property, leaving the low-lying features of the floodplain undisturbed. (See sidebar on Clinton County, Ohio, p. 55.)

WHERE HAZARDS FIT IN THE CIP

The Capital Improvements Program (CIP) lays out a jurisdiction's medium-term (five- to six-year) spending plan for capital projects that support existing and future development such as roadways and sewer and water systems. As such, it represents the locality's commitments to major expenditures and is concrete evidence of its priorities for implementing its policies and plans, including those for hazard mitigation.

There are two types of CIP commitments relevant to hazards: hazard-specific expenditures and the hazard-specific nonexpenditures. Specific relevant expenditures include spending for open space acquisition, such

---

(continued from page 52)

safety, and property because of their incompatible nature, location, design, or method of construction.

b. Require that uses and facilities vulnerable to geologic hazards be protected against collapse or severe damage at the time of construction or placement in the zone.

c. Control any fill, cut, construction or other development which may unnaturally increase the degree of hazards.

d. Require site-specific and building-specific studies by qualified engineering geologists, geological engineers, and building designers to adjust construction and land use to minimize the degree of hazard.

All structures and uses of land which are listed as permitted uses and permitted conditional uses in the underlying zoning districts shall also be permitted in the territory covered by the NHO Zone if they meet the standards of both this section and the underlying zone.

Before any building permit is issued within the NHO Zone, the Zoning Administrator must first find that the land use, grading, construction, or other such development to be permitted therein complies with both the requirements of the NHO Zone and the underlying zone and issue a written clearance attesting to such finding. No land use, grading, construction or other development shall be commenced or altered within the territory of the NHO Zone until the clearance and the building permit based on such clearance are granted.

Every application to use land, grade, construct, or otherwise develop in the NHO Zone shall be accompanied by a plot plan and construction plans required by Section 7-6 of this ordinance plus a Natural Hazards Assessment which complies with the standards of this chapter, unless exempted.

Source: http://planning.utah.gov/library/ Index_files/PDFs/ut5.12.pdf, sec. 5-12. ◄

SAN LUIS OBISPO COUNTY COASTAL HIGH-HAZARD AREAS

3. Coastal High Hazard areas.: The following requirements shall apply to new structures or any improvement / repair to an existing structure as specified in Subsection D., in areas identified as having special flood hazards extending from offshore to the inland limit of a primary frontal dune along an open coast and any other area subject to high velocity waters including coastal and tidal inundation or tsunamis as established on the maps identified in subsection A.:

a. All buildings or structures shall be elevated on adequately anchored pilings or columns and securely anchored to such pilings or columns so that the lowest horizontal portion of the structural members of the lowest floor (excluding the pilings or columns) is elevated to or above the base flood elevation level. The pile or column foundation and structure attached thereto is anchored to resist flotation, collapse, and lateral movement due to the effects of wind and water loads acting simultaneously on all building components. Water loading values used shall be those associated with the base flood. Wind loading values used shall be those required by applicable state or local building standards.

b. All new construction and other development shall be located on the landward side of the reach of mean high tide.

c. All buildings or structures shall have the space below the lowest floor free of obstructions or constructed with breakaway walls. Such enclosed space shall not be used for human habitation and will be usable solely for parking of vehicles, building access or storage.

d. Fill shall not be used for structural support of buildings.

e. Man-made alteration of sand dunes that would increase potential flood damage is prohibited.

f. The Director and / or the Public Works Director shall obtain and maintain the following records.

   (1) Certification by a registered engineer or architect that a proposed structure complies with Subsection D.3.a.

   (2) The elevation (in relation to mean sea level) of the bottom of the lowest structural member of the lowest floor (excluding pilings or columns) of all buildings and structures, and whether such structures contain a basement.

Source: www.slocounty.ca.gov/Assets/PL/Land+Use+Ordinances/ Title+22+-++Land+Use+Ordinance/01+-+Title+22+-+Land +Use+Ordinance+-+Article+1+through+8.pdf, sec. 22.14.060.

as at-risk waterfront properties that can be converted to public parks and greenways, and for hazard mitigation projects, such as strengthening at-risk public facilities—schools, hospitals, fire and police stations, utility systems—to resist floods and geologic hazards. (See sidebar on the King County Flood Control Zone District Proposed Work Program, p. 56).

Hazard-specific nonexpenditures include prohibitions against support of infrastructure projects that would increase the vulnerability of future development, such as extending trunk sewer lines into hazard areas or building bridges to barrier islands at risk from hurricanes and shoreline erosion. For example, the Lee County, Florida, comprehensive plan includes a statement limiting public expenditures in coastal high-hazard areas to necessary repairs, public safety needs, services to existing residents, recreation, and open space uses. (See Chapter 6.) It also prohibits new causeways to islands and bridges to undeveloped barrier islands, except to achieve evacuation clearance-time objectives.

TESTING IMPLEMENTATION WITH A SAFE GROWTH AUDIT

Beyond the use of individual planning implementation tools, hazards must be dealt with *comprehensively*, using complete packages of tools, in order to get the most effective result.

The *Safe Growth Audit* is a method to analyze how the full slate of current policies, ordinances, and plans on community safety affects hazard risks due to growth. The audit gives the community a comprehensive but concise evaluation of the positive and negative effects of its existing growth-guidance framework on future hazard vulnerability. It informs citizens and decision makers about important safety issues and highlights needed changes in policy and planning instruments (Godschalk 2009).

By answering a series of basic questions, the Safe Growth Audit can be used to test existing tools and policies, to involve stakeholders and decision makers in hazards issues, and to guide needed changes in growth-related tools. (See sidebar, p. 57.)

If the community and its elected officials understand how their zoning and subdivision ordinances allow growth in hazard areas, they can then revise those ordinances before property owners embark on risky projects. If they understand how their capital improvement programs encourage unsafe growth, they can then change their expenditure policies and priorities. For an example of action recommendations similar to those that might result from a Safe Growth Audit, see Kane County (2003, chap. 10).

Safe growth is community-specific. To define safe growth for a jurisdiction, consider its opposite, *unsafe growth*. Ask if accommodating the expected 20-year population growth according to the future land-use plan is likely to put more people in harm's way. Will it result in more intense development in known hazard areas? Will redevelopment policies increase the amount of

FROM THE CLINTON COUNTY, OHIO, SUBDIVISION REGULATIONS FOR CLUSTER AND CONSERVATION SUBDIVISIONS AND PLANNED UNIT DEVELOPMENT

410.00 PLANNED UNIT DEVELOPMENT
410.01.1 GENERAL STATEMENT
The Planned Unit Development is a contiguous area to be planned and developed as a single entity containing one or more structures to accommodate residential, commercial and / or industrial uses in accordance with the applicable zoning regulations. Zoning approval of a planned unit development does not constitute subdivision approval. The procedure for approval of a planned unit development is subject to the approval of these Regulations.

410.02 PURPOSE OF PLANNED UNIT DEVELOPMENT
A planned unit development of land may be permitted in order to provide a means for a more desirable physical development pattern than would not be possible through the strict application of zoning and subdivision regulations. The Regional Planning Commission will permit certain variety and flexibility in land development to encourage the subdivider to adjust design to irregular topography, economize in the construction of utilities, and create architectural variation as well as attractive and usable buildings and building sites.

410.03 GENERAL REQUIREMENTS
A. The gross area of the tract to be developed under the planned unit development approach shall comprise not less than ten (10) acres, unless otherwise approved by the Regional Planning Commission.

B. The total ground area occupied by buildings and structures shall not exceed eighty (80) percent of the total ground area, unless previous development in the neighborhood has a greater ground coverage, in which case the plan may increase the ground coverage of buildings and structures to correspond with the average in the neighborhood.

C. A minimum of ten (10) percent of the land developed shall be reserved for open space and similar uses such as an internal park network under these Regulations. Lot widths and required yards may be reduced to eighty (80) percent of the requirements of these Regulations.

D. The minimum lot size shall not be less than 70 percent of the lot area per family or use, which would otherwise be required under these Regulations. Lot widths and required yards may be reduced to 80 percent of the requirements of these Regulations.

E. The design of the internal circulation system shall provide for convenient access to dwelling units and non-residential facilities, separation of vehicular and pedestrian traffic, shall be adequate to carry anticipate traffic, including access for emergency vehicles.

420.00 CLUSTER OR CONSERVATION DEVELOPMENT
420.01 PURPOSE
A. It is the intent of this section to the Subdivision Regulations to be sufficiently flexible to carry out the conservation development objectives of the County. Conservation development is intended to encourage more efficient use of land and public services through unified development that is principally intended to conserve community resources, preserve open spaces, and protect the health and safety of the community. These objectives are achieved through land development techniques set forth in the Clinton County Zoning Resolution that permit flexibility in the arrangement and construction of dwelling units and roads. Therefore, this section establishes standards and criteria to likewise permit sufficient flexibility in the development of subdivisions to be consistent with the County's conservation development regulations, to maximize the achievement of the conservation development objectives and to promote the following purposes:

1. Minimize development on and destruction of sensitive natural resource areas;

2. Reduce the quantity and improve the quality of stormwater runoff from expected development;

3. Maintain natural characteristics such as woods, hedgerows, natural vegetation, meadows, and streams;

4. Reduce the amount of disturbed land and conservation of natural areas to landscaped areas for lawns and intrusive vegetation; and,

5. Maintain a traditional rural settlement pattern characterized by compact groupings of development in otherwise wide-open spaces.

Source: http://co.clinton.oh.us/regional_planning/clinton-county-subdivision-regulations-2006.pdf/view.

FROM THE KING COUNTY FLOOD CONTROL ZONE DISTRICT PROPOSED WORK PROGRAM

CAPITAL IMPROVEMENT PROGRAM IMPLEMENTATION

Program Summary: The vast majority of the proposed District work program and budget is dedicated to implementation of major maintenance and capital projects. This work includes managing and implementing major maintenance, repair and new flood protection facility design, permitting and construction projects; home buyouts and acquisitions; and home elevations.

Construction of flood protection infrastructure has allowed considerable residential, commercial and industrial economic development in flood hazard areas. The flood protection infrastructure has reduced the frequency of flooding and severity of erosion, and contained flood flows within levees that has allowed for significant economic growth by promoting development of historical floodplains, as exemplified by the industrial and commercial development lining the lower Green River. However, these areas will always face the potential risk that the flood protection facilities could be overwhelmed, resulting in serious flood damage, significant impacts to the regional economy, or personal injury and death. While the costs of flood protection facility construction and maintenance are borne by the public, the value to the economy is a regional benefit.

The Capital Improvement Program will complete high priority and regionally significant flood hazard management capital improvement projects to significantly protect public safety and reduce flood risks to the regional economy, transportation corridors, and public and private infrastructure and property. These capital improvement projects include retrofits and repairs to levees and revetments; levee setbacks to improve slope stability and increase flood conveyance and capacity; and targeted acquisition of repetitive loss properties and other at-risk developments. The District's Comprehensive Plan recommends approximately 135 capital projects for the ten-year period, of which approximately 95 are construction projects and 40 are acquisition only.

Source: www.kingcountyfloodcontrol.org/pdfs/2009%20kc%20flood%20 district%20work%20program.pdf

property vulnerable to hazard risks? Will the implementation of the capital improvement program encourage unsafe development proposals by facilitating access to dangerous locations? If unsafe growth appears likely, are there feasible land-use or regulatory alternatives that could be considered?

Safe growth is a straightforward concept. It can be summarized in a few simple principles (Beatley 2009, chap. 6):

Create a Safe Growth Vision. A safe growth strategy needs a vision of the future community safe from natural hazards. To create such a vision, institute a community dialogue about hazard exposure and vulnerability, coupled with frank discussion about the ways that growth is likely to increase risks. Acknowledge that public intervention may be necessary to mitigate risks and ask how existing plans, policies, and programs might be changed to accomplish such mitigation.

Guide Growth away from High-Risk Locations. A safe-growth analysis requires the use of maps of hazard areas. These high-risk locations—fault zones, flood zones, landslide hazard areas, erosion zones, wildfire zones—show where development should be discouraged or allowed only with special protections. Any public actions that ignore their impacts on development in such high-risk locations contribute to unsafe growth. Similarly, any public actions aimed at redevelopment in such locations should be scrutinized for increased risk.

Locate Critical Facilities Outside High-Risk Zones. Critical facilities need to be protected from hazard risks. Continued operation of water and sewer systems, roads and bridges, hospitals and medical facilities, power plants, and public safety facilities is critical to safe growth. Critical facilities in high-hazard zones not only pose a danger to their own operation but also put other development at risk. However, often it is necessary to locate such facilities in high-risk areas—for example, gravity-based sewage treatment plants must be built at low elevations and so may be subject to flooding—so protective measures must be incorporated into their designs.

Preserve Protective Features of the Natural Environment. Natural ecosystems need to be protected against unsafe growth practices. Removing vegetation from steep slopes for new buildings decreases the soil's ability to resist erosion and mud slides. Bulldozing mangroves for new beachfront projects decreases the ability of natural systems to absorb floodwaters. Filling riverine marshes for agriculture increases future flood flows.

Retrofit Buildings and Facilities at Risk in Redeveloping Areas. Redevelopment in existing areas needs to be protected against hazard risks. Many older buildings were built prior to building codes containing higher safety standards. Often, these areas also are located within hazard zones, as in the case of small beachfront communities. For them to accommodate higher densities and intensities of future development, their existing structures and facilities should be strengthened or elevated during the redevelopment process.

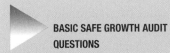

**BASIC SAFE GROWTH AUDIT
QUESTIONS**

COMPREHENSIVE PLAN

Land Use

- Does the future land-use map clearly identify natural-hazard areas?

- Do the land-use policies discourage development or redevelopment within natural-hazard areas?

- Does the plan provide adequate space for expected future growth in areas located outside of natural-hazard areas?

Transportation

- Does the transportation plan limit access to hazard areas?

- Is transportation policy used to guide growth to safe locations?

- Are movement systems designed to function under disaster conditions (e.g., evacuation)?

Environmental Management

- Are environmental systems that protect development from hazards identified and mapped?

- Do environmental policies maintain and restore protective ecosystems?

- Do environmental policies provide incentives to development that is located outside of protective ecosystems?

Public Safety

- Are the goals and policies of the comprehensive plan related to those of the FEMA Hazard Mitigation Plan?

- Is safety explicitly included in the plan's growth and development policies?

- Does the monitoring and implementation section of the plan cover safe-growth objectives?

ZONING ORDINANCE

- Does the zoning ordinance conform to the comprehensive plan in terms of discouraging development or redevelopment within natural hazard areas?

- Does the ordinance contain natural-hazard overlay zones that set conditions for land use within such zones?

- Do rezoning procedures recognize natural hazard areas as limits on zoning changes that allow greater intensity or density of use?

- Does the ordinance prohibit development within, or filling of, wetlands, floodways, and floodplains?

SUBDIVISION REGULATIONS

- Do the subdivision regulations restrict the subdivision of land within or adjacent to natural hazard areas?

- Do the regulations provide for conservation subdivisions or cluster subdivisions in order to conserve environmental resources?

- Do the regulations allow density transfers where hazard areas exist?

CAPITAL IMPROVEMENT PROGRAM AND INFRASTRUCTURE POLICIES

- Does the capital improvement program limit expenditures on projects that would encourage development in areas vulnerable to natural hazards?

- Do infrastructure policies limit extension of existing facilities and services that would encourage development in areas vulnerable to natural hazards?

- Does the capital improvement program provide funding for hazard mitigation projects identified in the FEMA Mitigation Plan?

OTHER

- Do small area or corridor plans recognize the need to avoid or mitigate natural hazards?

- Does the building code contain provisions to strengthen or elevate construction to withstand hazard forces?

- Do economic development or redevelopment strategies include provisions for mitigating natural hazards?

- Is there an adopted evacuation and shelter plan to deal with emergencies from natural hazards?

Source: Godschalk 2009

Develop Knowledgeable Community Leaders and Networks. Safe growth needs the knowledge and actions of all community stakeholders, including nongovernmental institutions and social networks. Governments alone cannot ensure safe growth. Thus, a Safe Growth Audit needs to look at how community stakeholders share knowledge about hazards and make decisions relative to growth. The goal is to ensure strong community networks and community leaders prepared to make safe decisions concerning growth both before and after disasters.

Monitor and Update Safe Growth Programs and Plans. Safe growth needs up-to-date programs and plans. Natural hazard and vulnerability estimates change as new information becomes available from updated analyses and as the result of learning from disasters. Growth conditions also change, as new development trends emerge and new projections are made. Safe Growth Audits should be revised and publicly reviewed on a regular basis to ensure their continued validity, in conjunction with scheduled updates to the comprehensive plan and hazard mitigation plan.

NOTES

1. Building codes set engineering standards for building safety in the face of hazard stresses. They are administered by local governments, but they are written and revised by building-code councils. For example, the International Code Council (ICC) publishes the International Building Code, the American Society of Civil Engineers (ASCE) publishes *Minimum Design Standards for Buildings and Other Structures* (ASCE 7-02), and the National Fire Protection Association publishes the Fire Code. Some states also publish building codes. For a general overview, see the *Whole Building Design Guide*, National Institute of Building Sciences, available at www.wbdg.org/design/resist_hazards.php.

2. The California Natural Hazards Disclosure Act requires that sellers of real property and their agents provide prospective buyers with a "Natural Hazard Disclosure Statement" when the property being sold lies within one or more state-mapped hazard areas. These seismic hazard zone maps are distributed to local governments for use in planning and controlling construction and development. These regulatory zones encompass areas prone to liquefaction (failure of water-saturated soil) and earthquake-induced landslides. If a property is undeveloped, a site-specific investigation by a licensed engineering geologist or civil engineer may be required before the parcel can be subdivided or before most structures can be permitted. If a significant hazard exists at the site, then measures must be recommended to reduce the risk to an acceptable level. See www.consrv.ca.gov/CGS/shzp/Pages/SHMPrealdis.aspx.

3. California's Senate Bill 375 (2008) seeks to reduce greenhouse gas emissions by curbing urban sprawl, reducing commute times, and encouraging infill development. Essentially a growth management law that ties transportation funding to growth patterns, the bill requires each California region to create a preferred growth scenario that will enable it to meet regional greenhouse gas–reduction targets derived from the statewide reduction goal. Each metropolitan planning organization (MPO) must prepare a "sustainable communities strategy," which will be the land-use allocation in the regional transportation plan. The strategy is to identify land-use patterns and housing needs and set forth a forecasted development pattern, which when integrated with the transportation network and policies will reduce greenhouse gas emissions from automobiles and light trucks to achieve the approved reduction targets. Implementation is delegated to the regions, and land-use regulation authority remains with the cities and counties.

CHAPTER 6

Case Studies: Large Jurisdictions

In testing ideas about how planning *should* operate with regard to natural hazards and the integration of hazard mitigation into local planning, we need to assess how well planning *does* operate. Planning is seldom a simple enterprise because it is influenced by politics, social considerations, economics, physical geography, and numerous other factors that make up the daily life of any community.

In searching for a representative range of communities that have made sustained efforts to integrate hazard mitigation into planning, APA's project team, in cooperation with FEMA personnel, considered more than 50 candidates. The case studies in this chapter and the next two focus on places of varying size, circumstances, and geography. In every instance we tried to learn what factors and people drove whatever success these communities have achieved.

This case study focuses on the following documents:

- *Joint Unified Local Mitigation Strategy for Lee County, Florida* (2007), which fulfills the state and federal local hazard-mitigation plan requirement

- *The Lee Plan* (2007) and the February 25, 2009, Amendment to the Hurricane Evacuation/Coastal High Hazard Area

- *Lee County Master Mitigation Plan (Environmental Quality Investment and Growth Mitigation Strategic Plan)* (2007)

Mitigation documents describing the State of Florida's natural-hazard mitigation plan and local mitigation guidelines are also reviewed.

The following officials reviewed this case study, to ensure the accuracy of its description and interpretation:

- John Wilson, Lee County Public Safety Director

- Mary Gibbs, AICP, Lee County Community Development Director

- Bill Spikowski, AICP, planning consultant and former director of the Lee County Growth Management Department

LEE COUNTY, FLORIDA
David R. Godschalk, FAICP

A low-lying county facing the Gulf of Mexico, Lee County faces significant natural hazards of flooding and hurricanes, as well as wildfires, tornadoes, thunderstorms, and other hazards. In attempting to remedy the impacts of decades of urbanization on its natural environment while also managing continued growth, the county has adopted a collaborative Joint Unified Local Mitigation Strategy that coordinates mitigation for the county and its five municipalities. The strategy is integrated with the comprehensive plans of all the jurisdictions and is implemented through development regulation, as well as through governmental expenditures. The county's approach can be viewed as a model for dealing with coastal hazards in urbanized counties with significant natural areas.

Purpose and Method
Because the unified strategy brings together the mitigation efforts of the county and its five municipalities, it can serve as a model for regional coordination. Additionally, because it directly integrates hazard mitigation and the local comprehensive plans, it can be viewed as a model for integration of mitigation into comprehensive planning. Last, because it carries out hazard mitigation through both development regulations and governmental expenditures, the strategy can be viewed as a model for prioritizing and implementing mitigation initiatives through such tools. This collaborative strategy has both strengths and problems.

Florida governments are required to prepare five plans (or parts of plans) that involve mitigation and land use:

- *Local Comprehensive Plan*—a local policy plan defining future land-use and growth patterns

- *Coastal Element of the Comprehensive Plan*—a section of the comprehensive plan focusing on protection of the coastal environment and communities from natural hazards

- *County Comprehensive Emergency Management Plan* (CEMP)—an operational plan defining emergency management procedures

- *Local Mitigation Strategy*—a plan required by both the state and the federal government

- *Postdisaster Redevelopment Plan*—a plan for the postdisaster recovery period

Background: Hazards, Geography, and Institutions
The context for hazard mitigation planning—natural hazards, geographic setting, and regulatory environment—sets the context for mitigation implementation. Lee County faces significant natural hazards and occupies a low-lying environment with large areas of wetlands. In response, it has created agencies and procedures to mitigate its hazards, conserve its environmental resources, and manage its future development.

Lee County lies on the southwest Gulf Coast of Florida. As seen in Figure 6.1, the county includes five municipalities: Fort Myers, Fort Myers Beach, Sanibel, Cape Coral, and Bonita Springs. It is split by the Caloosahatchee River, which flows west from Lake Okeechobee into the Gulf of Mexico, and it has an extensive shoreline, exposing all of its urban areas to the threat of flooding.

Hurricanes, tropical storms, and drought are the major natural hazards in Lee County, along with thunderstorms, tornadoes, floods, and wildfires.

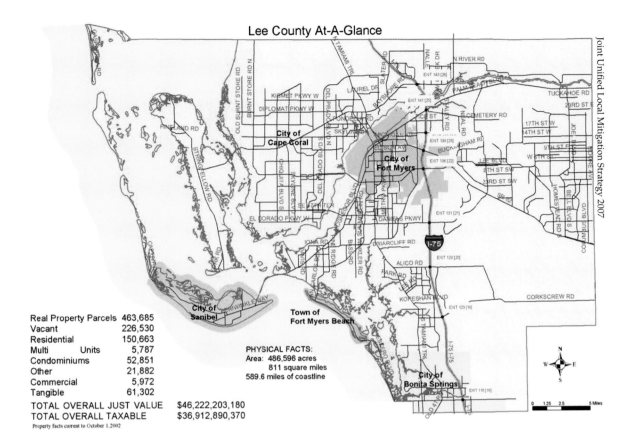

Figure 6.1. *Lee County map*

According to the county's 2007 Hazard Vulnerability Analysis, hurricanes, tropical coastal storms, tropical cyclone events, and drought affect the largest population—615,741, the total population of the county at that time (Lee County Division of Emergency Management 2007). Other natural-hazard impacts include those from storm surge events affecting 532,589, thunderstorms and tornadoes affecting 18,096, floods affecting 13,490, and wildfires affecting 7,047. (See Table 6.1.)

Lee County's natural environment—consisting of 804 square miles of land and 408 square miles of coastal and inland waters—is extremely sensitive (Lee County Board of County Commissioners 2007). Historic development has fragmented aquatic systems, destroyed upland areas, and filled or drained freshwater, saltwater, and tidal wetlands. In the process, water-retention and drought-buffering capacities have been lost, along with wildlife habitat. Freshwater and estuarine systems have been listed as "impaired" by the Florida Department of Environmental Protection (DEP). This is important to hazard mitigation since these natural systems are the first line of defense against coastal flooding, storm surge, and drought.

Lee County's hazard mitigation and planning agencies operate within the federal/state/local hierarchy of governments. Because the natural environment is critical to hazard mitigation and because urban development determines which areas will be subject to hazards, this hierarchy includes environmental management and comprehensive planning agencies, as well as emergency management agencies.

TABLE 6.1. 2007 HAZARD VULNERABILITY ANALYSIS

Hazard Description	Is Event Significant	Frequency			Maximum Population Affected
		1 year	5 year	10 year	
Agricultural Freeze	Y		X		22,815
Air Transportation Accident	Y		X		11,961
Bridge Failure	Y			>	0
Brush Fires, Wildfires, and Forest Fires	Y	X			
Civil Disturbance	Y				10,695
Commercial Nuclear Power Plant Incidents	N				0
Critical Infrastructure Disruption (Computer Threat, Gas Pipeline Disruption)					
Drought	Y		X		615,741
Exotic Pest and Disease (Mediterranean fruit flies, citrus canker, red rings disease)	Y			X	26,842
Extreme Temperatures					
Flood (Major)	Y		X		13,490
Flood (Minor)	Y	X			1,127
Fixed Facility, Hazardous Material	Y		X		250,036
Oil Spill, Hazardous Coastal Material	Y		X		------
Highway Accident, Hazardous Material	Y	X			217,452
Rail Accident, Hazardous Material	Y			X	228,329
River, Hazardous Material	Y	X			228,901
Hurricane / Tropical Storm	Y		X		615,741
Major Transportation Incidents					------
Mass Immigration	Y			>	13,000
Nuclear Attack	Y				615,741
Pandemic Disease Outbreaks	Y				532,589
Power Failure	Y	X			126,086
Radiological Incident, Transportation	Y		X		1,425
Severe Thunderstorms	Y	X			1,414
Sinkholes and Subsidence	N				------
Special Events (dignitary visits, spring break, etc.)	N	X			------

(continued on page 63)

(continued from page 62)

TABLE 6.1. 2007 HAZARD VULNERABILITY ANALYSIS (*CONTINUED*)

Hazard Description	Is Event Significant	Frequency			Maximum Population Affected
		1 year	5 year	10 year	
Tropical Cyclone Events, Storm Surge	Y	X			532,589
Tropical Cyclone Events, Wind	Y	X			615,741
Terrorism	Y			X	198,624
Thunderstorms and Tornadoes	Y	X			18,096
Urban Fire	Y	X			1,414
Wildfire	Y	X			7,047

Note: > means occurrence is greater than 10 years
Source: Joint Unified Local Mitigation Strategy 2007

The primary federal hazards agency is FEMA. However, the U.S. Army Corps of Engineers, the U.S. Environmental Protection Agency, and the U.S. Department of Interior Fish and Wildlife Service also play important roles in Lee County.

At the state level, the Florida Department of Community Affairs (DCA) directs comprehensive planning. DCA administers the Florida Growth Management Act, a prescriptive, top-down approach in which state laws and regulations set out explicit requirements governing the scope of local comprehensive plan goals, objectives, and policies (Deyle, Chapin, and Baker 2008). Regulations adopted by DCA require coastal counties and municipalities to adopt comprehensive plan objectives and policies that limit development in and direct population away from Coastal High Hazard Areas (storm surge zones for Category 1 hurricanes) and maintain or reduce evacuation times within hurricane vulnerability zones (areas that would be evacuated for a Category 3 hurricane).

The Florida Division of Emergency Management (DEM), now in the Office of the Governor but formerly a division within DCA, administers FEMA hazard-mitigation funding programs, oversees preparation of county comprehensive emergency-management plans, oversees the preparation and review of local hazard-mitigation plans, and maintains the state hazard-mitigation plan.

The Florida DEP, Fish and Wildlife Conservation Commission, and Department of Transportation also play important roles in both planning and hazard mitigation.

DCA's guide for local mitigation planning, *Florida Local Mitigation Strategy* (State of Florida n.d.), recommends policies that:

- limit public expenditures in repetitive damage areas;

- protect critical facilities;

- remove and relocate damaged and vulnerable infrastructure;

- eliminate development in hazard-prone areas;

- regulate nonconforming land uses;

- regulate land use, beach and dune alteration, floodplains, nonpoint-source runoff, and sanitary sewers and septic tanks in hazard-prone areas;

- prioritize coastal areas for water-dependent uses;

- encourage removal of septic tanks and hazardous sites;

- regulate watershed alteration;

- encourage economic diversification;

- prioritize property for acquisition;

- address repetitively damaged structures;

- identify policies for poststorm reconstruction;

- review application for funding for concurrence with mitigation objectives; and

- establish a working group to direct mitigation initiatives.

At the regional level, the South Florida Water Management District has regulatory and water-resource management responsibilities. The Southwest Florida Regional Planning Council is a six-county regional planning agency charged with protecting and improving the region's social, physical, and economic environment. However, it has no regulatory authority.

At the county level, the primary hazard mitigation agency is the Lee County Public Safety Division. In addition to its emergency management program, the division operates the 9-1-1 program, the emergency medical-services program, an emergency telecommunications program, a logistical support program, and a public information program, and it also provides fire protection services to dependent districts. For response operation purposes, the county is divided into 10 Disaster Response Divisions (Figure 6.2).

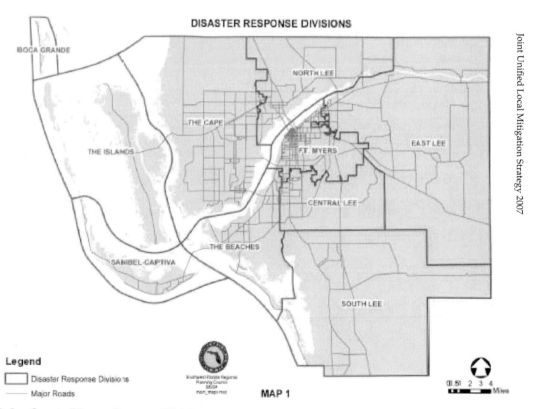

Figure 6.2. Lee County Disaster Response Divisions

The primary planning agency is the Lee County Department of Community Development, which maintains and updates the Lee Plan. Its responsibilities include not only monitoring and evaluating the plan but also processing amendments to it and implementing its goals, objectives, policies, and standards through the county zoning and development review processes, which are required to be consistent with it. Divisions within the department include Planning (land-use plan, housing, and historic preservation), Development Services (plan review, permitting, and rezoning), Environmental Sciences, Building Inspections, and Code Enforcement.

Hazard Mitigation

The Joint Unified Local Mitigation Strategy (LMS) seeks to lessen the human, economic, and environmental costs resulting from large-scale natural hazards (Local Mitigation Strategy Work Group 2007). It is a plan to promote mitigation from hazards posing a threat to communities within Lee County and a tool to establish funding priorities for disaster assistance following a major disaster. It is structured to comply with Lee Plan Policy 110.1.5, which states that the county shall maintain the floodplain management plan that assesses the flooding problem of unincorporated areas, inventories flood hazard areas, reviews possible activities to remedy flooding problems, selects appropriate alternatives, and formulates an implementation schedule. It is tied directly to policies contained in the Lee County Comprehensive Emergency Management Plan (CEMP), as well as to the Lee Plan, and it includes the Lee Plan Future Land Use Map and other specific linkages. For example, Objective 1.1 of the LMS states that preventive activities shall be governed by the Lee Plan and the Lee County Land Development Code. Similarly, Objective 1.7 is to continue supporting the Lee Plan, while many other objectives seek to maintain natural resources and systems identified in the Lee Plan.

The LMS assesses the vulnerability to and risk from various types of hazards on a parcel-by-parcel basis, identifies plans and programs to lessen the effects of disasters, and implements the strategy, which is necessary to secure pre- and postdisaster federal mitigation grant funding, support pre- and postdisaster decision making, and identify and rank mitigation initiatives across all county and municipal agencies.

The LMS planning process was conducted by the legally adopted Lee County Disaster Advisory Council, which serves as the Local Mitigation Strategy Workgroup. Chaired by the public safety director, the workgroup includes:

- County department heads
- Community representatives
- Municipal government liaisons
- School and independent fire district representatives
- Regional governmental bodies
- Others appointed by the Lee County Commission

The workgroup solicited public comments, contacted other agencies, and reviewed existing plans, reports, and technical information. It then prepared the strategy, including a detailed statement of goals and objectives and a prioritized list of mitigation initiatives.

The overall goal of the strategy is to develop and maintain a hazard-resistant community. Its seven specific goals, each with multiple objectives, are to:

- Reduce risk to life and damage to property
- Reduce damage to repetitively damaged properties

- Preserve or maintain natural areas
- Support emergency services
- Obtain funding for engineered projects
- Provide public information
- Maintain pre- and postdisaster redevelopment and mitigation policies

The workgroup created a prioritized list of mitigation initiatives from plans, programs, and projects identified during the risk analysis. It developed criteria and assigned numerical scores, using a ranking worksheet. Initiative ranking criteria were:

- Presence in community comprehensive plans, programs, and policies
- Consistency with existing regulatory framework
- Probability of funding (with local funds)
- Community Rating System credit
- Community benefit
- Community exposure to identified hazard
- Level of public demand, countywide
- Complexity of implementation
- Estimated ratio of benefit to cost
- Critical services improvement
- Time frame to complete project

The final table of ranked initiatives characterizes them by community, estimated cost, eligibility for federal Hazard Mitigation Grant Program (HMGP) funding, initiative completion or status, and the goal and objective met.

The risk assessment includes four main components: hazard identification, profiles of hazard events, asset inventory, and potential loss estimation. While the risk assessment looks at Lee County as a whole, it also singles out specific areas of special concern, including historic structures (Figure 6.3), top 100 employers (Figure 6.4), target neighborhoods with an 80 percent or greater concentration of below-poverty-level households that may have special needs in the event of a disaster (Figure 6.5), and critical facilities, infrastructure, and lifelines (Figure 6.6). Each of these focus areas is mapped relative to the Disaster Response Divisions.

Comprehensive Planning

All Florida local governments are required to adopt comprehensive plans under chapter 163 of the Florida Statutes. The plans serve three broad purposes. First, certain public and private activities within each jurisdiction must be consistent with the goals, objectives, and policies in the adopted plans. Second, the plans provide authority for local governments' land-development regulations and official actions, such as zoning ordinances and capital improvement programs. Finally, the plans represent the communities' vision of what they should look like by the end of the planning horizon.

The Lee County vision is designed to depict the county in 2030. It projects an increase in population to 979,000 permanent residents, with an additional 18 percent increase in seasonal residents (Lee County DCD 2009a, I-1). Its themes are:

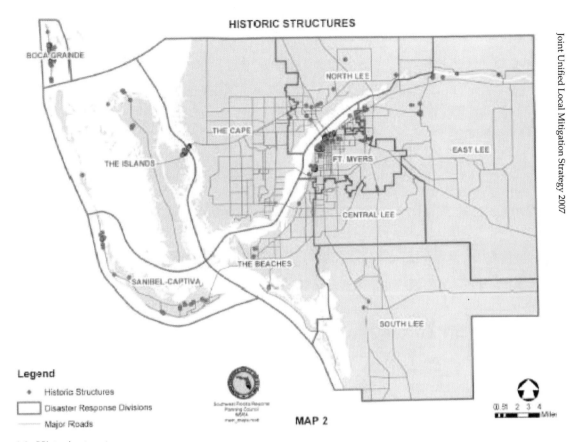

Figure 6.3. Historic structures

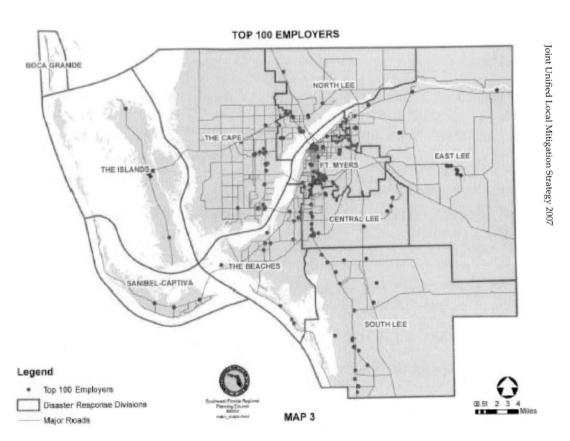

Figure 6.4. Top 100 employers

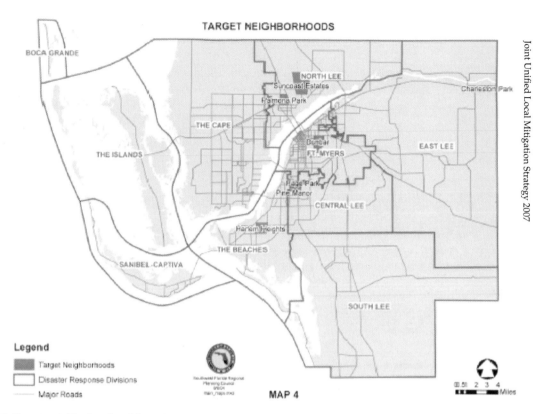

Figure 6.5. Target neighborhoods with an 80 percent or greater concentration of low-income, below-poverty-level households

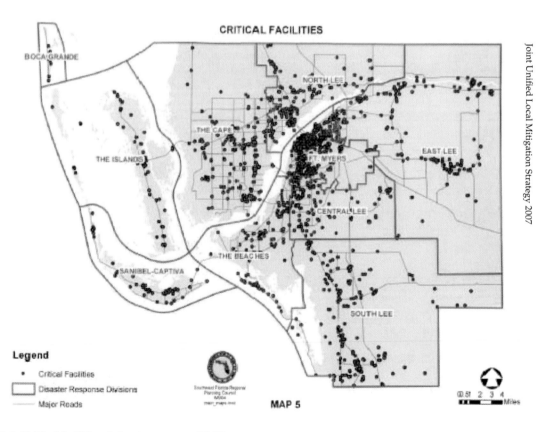

Figure 6.6. Critical facilities, infrastructure, and lifelines

- Growth patterns will be dictated by the Future Land Use Map (FLUM), which will not change dramatically during the plan's time frame. The urban area will be essentially built out by 2030, with the exception of Cape Coral and Lehigh Acres (a large unincorporated subdivision) and some potential redevelopment. The success of the plan in distinguishing between urban and rural areas will depend upon the continuing viability of agriculture and the amount of publicly owned land in outlying areas.

- The county will protect its natural resource base through public land acquisition and enforcing land-use and environmental regulations that supplement federal, state, and regional regulatory programs.

- The traditional economic base will be diversified to increase high-paying jobs, reduce residents' tax burdens, and enhance community stability. Agriculture, commercial fishing, tourism, and construction will continue to be significant but will become less important in relation to new business opportunities afforded by the expanded international airport and the new university.

- Cultural, educational, and recreational opportunities will expand as the result of the county's increased urbanization.

- Increased urbanization will require investment in physical and social infrastructure. Public facilities will be maintained at adequate levels of service, both by construction of new facilities and by conserving capacity of existing facilities. Social problems will be addressed by early intervention and other programs.

- The Lee Plan's land-use accommodation is based on an aggregation of allocations for 22 Planning Communities, which are planning subdistricts designed to capture the character of individual areas of the county.

In addition to the Vision Statement, the Lee Plan contains elements addressing specific functions, including Future Land Use; Transportation; Community Facilities and Services; Parks, Recreation, and Open Space; Capital Improvements; and others. In terms of natural-hazard mitigation, the most significant element is chapter 7, on conservation and coastal management, which contains 128 goals, most related to critical environmental conservation issues but seven particularly focused on mitigation. Specific natural-hazard mitigation goals, as well as more general conservation and coastal management goals, of this element are:

> Goal 101: Planning, coordination, and implementation
>
> Goal 102: People with special needs
>
> Goal 105: Protection of life and property in coastal high-hazard areas
>
> Goal 106: Limitation of public expenditures in coastal high-hazard areas
>
> Goal 109: Evacuation and shelter
>
> Goal 110: Hazard mitigation
>
> Goal 111: Postdisaster redevelopment

Goal 101: Planning, Coordination, and Implementation. Under this goal, objective 101.1 states that the county will maintain a system that protects the population at risk of injury or death from the natural and technological hazards defined in the Lee County Hazard Vulnerability Analysis. This objective is supported with policies that state that: (1) the Comprehensive Emergency Management Plan will be the operational guide for hazard preparation, response, and recovery; (2) the county will implement an education and information program on the risks of hazards and their mitigation; (3) the county will maintain facilities and sites for emergency assistance; and (4) the county will coordinate the development of emergency plans and programs among governments, Florida Gulf Coast University, and other agencies.

Goal 102: People with Special Needs. Under this goal, objective 102.1 states that the county will have mechanisms to assist people with special needs during an emergency. This objective is supported with policies that require (1) new hospitals, nursing homes, adult congregate living facilities, or projects for the developmentally disabled to prepare emergency preparedness plans; (2) the county to assist in emergency transportation needs of residents with limited mobility; and (3) the county to continue to provide basic medical services in shelters for people with special needs.

Goal 105: Protection of Life and Property in Coastal High-Hazard Areas. Objective 105.1, development in coastal high-hazard areas, states that: (1) new development on barrier islands will be limited to densities that meet required evacuation standards; (2) new development requiring seawalls for protection from coastal erosion will not be permitted; and (3) allowable densities for undeveloped areas in coastal high-hazard areas will be considered for reduction. This objective is further amplified through policies relating to barrier island densities, use of natural vegetation, setbacks and beach renourishment rather than hardened structures, and limits on future populations exposed to coastal flooding.

Goal 106: Limitation of Public Expenditures in Coastal High-Hazard Areas. Objective 106.1, coastal high-hazard expenditures, states that public expenditures in areas subject to repeated destruction by hurricanes will be limited to necessary repairs, public safety needs, services to existing residents, recreation, and open space uses. This objective is supported with policies requiring findings by the county commission that such expenditures are necessary and prohibiting new causeways to any islands and new bridges to undeveloped barrier islands except to achieve evacuation clearance-time objectives.

Goal 109: Evacuation and Shelter. Objective 109.1, evacuation (as amended in 2009), states that by 2030 Lee County will work toward attaining a level of service for out-of-county hurricane evacuation for a Category 5 storm event that does not exceed 18 hours (16 hours for plan amendments in the coastal high-hazard area). This objective is supported with policies requiring:

- assessment of the impact of new development on hurricane evacuation and mitigation through either structural (on-site or off-site shelter) or nonstructural methods;

- updates of the hurricane evacuation portion of the CEMP to be coordinated with computer transportation modeling to identify critical roadway links;

- assignment of high priority for capital improvement expenditures to critical roadway links causing congestion on evacuation routes;

- design and construction of bridges on evacuation routes to accommodate needs of both auto and marine traffic; and

- comprehensive plan amendments that decrease density within coastal high-hazard areas to meet specific evacuation and shelter criteria.

The county adopted land-development regulations addressing hurricane preparedness and requiring mitigation measures that offset development impacts on hurricane evacuation and shelter (Lee County Land Development Regulations II.XI).

Objective 109.2, shelter, states that by 2010 adequate shelter space will be available for the population in the Hurricane Vulnerability Zone at risk under a Category 3 storm. This objective is supported with policies that (1) state the basis for shelter demand as 10 percent of the population at risk in the Hurricane Vulnerability Zone under a Category 5 storm hazard scenario; and (2) require the county to implement a program to meet this level of service by 2030, to meet standards for on-site shelters, and to determine the feasibility of using vertical shelters.

Goal 110: Hazard Mitigation. Objective 110.1, development regulations, states that all development regulations will be reviewed and revised to require a reduction of the vulnerability of future development in the FEMA A-Zone. This objective is supported with policies that state that:

- regulations and incentives will be examined for additional setbacks in critical erosion areas, conservation of dunes and vegetation, flood-proofing of utilities, and structural wind resistance and floodplain management;

- new or expanded mobile home or recreational vehicle development will not be permitted on barrier islands or in V-Zones;

- new residential development of more than 50 units must provide information on hurricane evacuation and shelter locations, and that of more than 100 units must formulate an emergency hurricane-preparedness plan;

- the county will analyze alternatives to solve flooding problems and formulate a schedule for implementation;

- the county will maintain the provision of the Flood Management Ordinance that holds that the 50 percent improvement threshold is cumulative for repetitive loss properties;

- the county will maintain the regulation requiring that any repetitive loss property that is improved by more than 25 percent of its replacement value must be brought into compliance with current regulatory standards.

Goal 111: Postdisaster Redevelopment. Objective 111.1, postdisaster strategic plan, states that the county will maintain institutions and procedures to guide county actions following a natural or technological disaster. This objective is supported with policies to maintain a Recovery Task Force and guidelines for determining acquisition priorities for storm-damaged property in hazard-prone areas, to establish principles for repairing or relocating public facilities in hazard-prone areas, and to modify the CEMP to contain details for postdisaster recovery.

Objective 111.2, postdisaster ordinance, states that an ordinance will be maintained to implement the Post-Disaster Strategic Plan (see the Lee County Post-Disaster Recovery Ordinance: www.lee-county.com/gov/bocc/ordinances/Ordinances/07-20.pdf). This objective is supported with policies that the ordinance will provide for enactment of a temporary moratorium on rebuilding, that it may incorporate a redevelopment plan for hazard-prone areas, and that it will implement the county build-back policy, which states that damaged structures whose reconstruction cost exceeds 50 percent of their replacement value may be rebuilt at their original size and type only if they comply with all federal, state, and local regulations, including elevation above the 100-year flood level.

Finally, the Future Land Use Map is included in both the Lee Plan and in the Joint Unified Local Mitigation Strategy for Lee County. The Future Land Use Map specifies the location and type of all areas of land use for the planning period. It is the touchstone for regulation of future development and conservation in the county. The extensive amounts of Non-Urban Areas and Environmentally Critical Areas (Wetlands) shown in various shades of green on the map also tend to coincide with many of the hazard areas in the county. (See Figure 6.7.) That it is published in both the comprehensive plan and the hazard mitigation plan is a strong indicator of the coordination of these plans.

Both in terms of broad goals and specific objectives and policies, the county's planning and emergency management divisions are on the same page. There can be no doubt that the leaders of these organizations have worked together over time to formulate and coordinate their respective plans. The next question is: Do they work together to implement the plans?

Integrated Implementation Techniques

Guided by adopted goals, objectives, and policies, plan implementation in Lee County is accomplished through a variety of means, ranging from day-to-day decisions to public expenditures to regulatory enforcement. Effective implementation requires a multi- and intradepartmental approach. For example, Planning works with Public Safety to write and revise the major policies, but implementation of those policies is carried out through zoning, building and site plan review, and permitting and development review. Use of procedures in the Land Development Code and safeguards, such as site plan review checklists, ensures that critical issues are not overlooked. Because the most effective way to keep future county residents out of harm's way is through development regulations that limit growth in high-hazard areas, enforcement of those regulations is a cost-effective, ongoing means of implementing natural-hazard mitigation.

For example, a recent planning staff letter explains why the North River Village development proposal failed to meet the hazard mitigation intent of the Lee Plan: "Planning staff is concerned that the request is counter to the intent of the *Lee Plan* as expressed in the Conservation and Coastal Management element Goal 105, Objective 105.1, and Policy 105.1.4. Goal 105 seeks to protect human life and developed property from natural disasters. Objective 105.1, in part, provides that allowable densities for undeveloped areas within coastal high-hazard areas will be considered for reduction" (Lee County DCD 2008). The letter notes that Policy 105.1.4 states that future land-use designations of undeveloped areas within coastal high-hazard areas will be considered, through the plan amendment process, for reduced density categories in order to limit the future population exposed to coastal flooding. It points out that the applicant is seeking to double the density on a site with substantial lands within the Coastal High Hazard Area, which is inconsistent with the intent of the Lee Plan policy. The development proposal was later withdrawn.

Lessons Learned

Lee County offers important lessons for integrating natural-hazard mitigation strategy and comprehensive planning.

- By bringing together mitigation for the county and its five municipalities into a unified plan, the strategy offers a model for regional (countywide) coordination. The Unified Local Mitigation Strategy was prepared by the Local Mitigation Strategy Workgroup, made up of representatives from each municipality, as well as the county and other relevant agencies. Each municipality's vulnerabilities and mitigation needs were explicitly recognized in the strategy, along with those of the overall county.

- By directly integrating the hazard mitigation strategy and the local comprehensive plan, the strategy offers a model for integration of mitigation into comprehensive planning. Goals and objectives of the strategy and the plan complement one another, with clear references to relevant activities and programs.

- By carrying out hazard mitigation through both governmental expenditures and development regulations, the strategy offers a model for prioritizing and

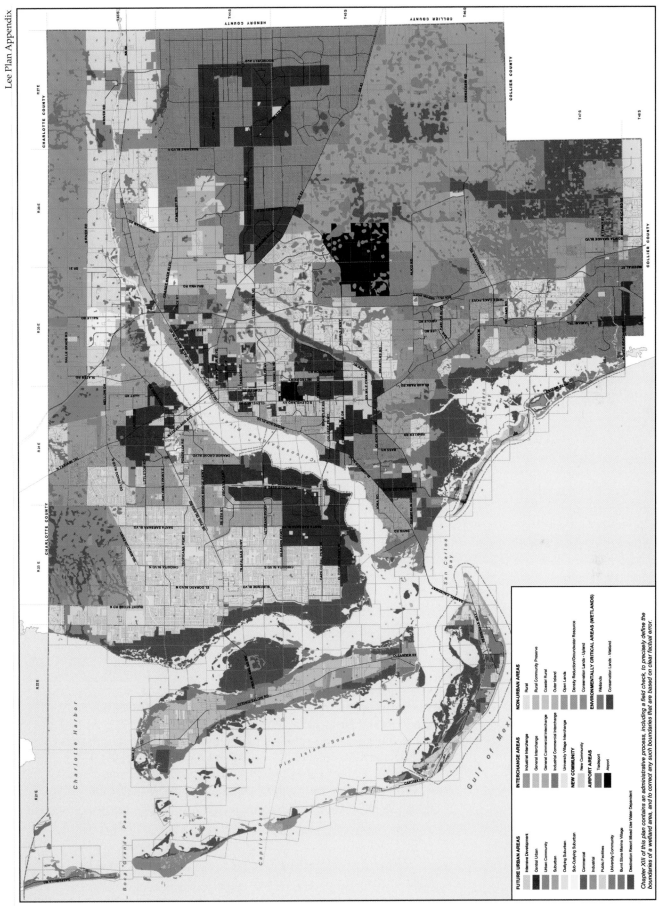

Figure 6.7. *Future land use map*

implementing mitigation initiatives. The workgroup ranks the mitigation initiatives, which are recognized in and implemented through the capital expenditure programs of the individual governments, ensuring local buy-in. Mitigation is also implemented on an ongoing basis through development plan reviews and regulations, ensuring that all rezoning and land-development applications, down to the level of building permits, are systematically evaluated against the plan policies, goals, and objectives. Each rezoning and site plan approval request is assessed by the county planning staff for compliance with the goals of the comprehensive plan, including those that pertain to mitigation as well as to future development in general.

An additional lesson has to do with the importance of history and consistent leadership to the success of the county's emergency management and planning operations. Emergency management and community development coordination goes back to the Lee County 1979 Hurricane Evacuation Plan, which identified the hurricane safety problem as a growth issue, based on the pioneering efforts of the City of Sanibel to set a carrying-capacity-based growth cap linked to evacuation capacity. It led to regional evacuation studies using SLOSH (Sea, Lake and Overland Surges from Hurricanes, a computerized model run by the National Hurricane Center to estimate storm surge heights and winds) to define the hurricane hazard.

Lee County has benefited from continuing leadership in planning and emergency management since adoption of the 1989 Lee Plan. Champions have included: Porter Goss, former mayor of Sanibel and chair of the County Commission; Wayne Daltry, executive director of the Southwest Florida Regional Planning Council; Mary Gibbs, community development director, who was previously a staff planner at the Regional Council; and John Wilson, Public Safety Department director, who is trained in both emergency management and comprehensive planning (a rare but valuable combination). All championed the cause of planning keyed to hazard mitigation. When Goss became chair of the Lee County Commission, he built on his experience as mayor during adoption of the Sanibel Plan to spark the preparation of the 1989 Lee Plan with its explicit environmental policies. Daltry and Gibbs applied their knowledge from earlier regional evacuation work to continuing planning and emergency management at the county level. And Wilson used his background in comprehensive planning to craft mitigation policies for the Lee Plan's land-use element.

A final lesson is that even the most comprehensive and collaborative natural-hazard mitigation and comprehensive planning policies cannot completely overturn years of previous unwise development actions. Many of the policies in the Lee Plan and the Unified Local Mitigation Strategy are aimed at attempting to repair historic zoning decisions that allowed development in the high-hazard areas. As research has shown, this is a lesson for Florida as a whole and other states; planning mandates aimed at managing development in critical areas may have marginal effects because of prior entitlements and the legal and political inertia of previous plans and land-development regulations (Deyle, Chapin, and Baker 2008). It is difficult to undo the impacts of decades of unsafe development practices.

On balance, the Lee County approach offers a model collaborative process and a set of mitigation and comprehensive plan policies whose integration could not be more complete.

CHARLOTTE-MECKLENBURG COUNTY, NORTH CAROLINA
Joseph MacDonald, AICP

Over the past several decades, Charlotte-Mecklenburg County, North Carolina, has experienced rapid growth and both the positive and negative consequences of it. Located in the Piedmont of south-central North Carolina, Mecklenburg

County is bordered on the west by the Catawba River, on the north by Iredell County, on the east by Cabarrus and Union counties, and on the south by South Carolina. Mecklenburg County contains seven municipalities: the City of Charlotte and the towns of Cornelius, Davidson, Huntersville, Matthews, Mint Hill, and Pineville. (See Figure 6.8.) As they grew, Mecklenburg County and the City of Charlotte became functionally, though not politically, consolidated. Charlotte extends its operational responsibilities and assigns many remaining responsibilities to Mecklenburg County through interlocal service agreements (Mead 2000). Since the mid-1990s, all significant public services have been offered countywide by either the City of Charlotte or Mecklenburg County (known as Charlotte-Mecklenburg). The six other towns may opt out of such services; five of six elect to provide their own law enforcement.

The dramatic spread of urban development has increased Charlotte-Mecklenburg's vulnerability to hazards in two ways: (1) a higher number of people and properties at risk; and (2) altered location, frequency, and intensity of hazards, particularly flooding. As a result, Charlotte-Mecklenburg staff, officials, and stakeholders have collaborated to mitigate the impacts of those hazards. This case study examines their initiatives to identify both current and future hazard vulnerability, establish strong collaborative partnerships to solve hazard mitigation problems, and integrate hazard mitigation planning into other objectives, such as water-quality protection, parks and recreation planning, and comprehensive planning policy.

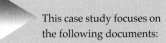

This case study focuses on the following documents:

- *Mecklenburg County Floodplain Guidance Management Document* (1997)

- *Charlotte-Mecklenburg Surface Water Improvement Management (SWIM) Implementation Guidelines* (2000)

- Post-Construction Storm Water Ordinance (2007)

- *Administrative Manual for Implementation of the Post-Construction Storm Water Ordinance* (2008)

- Mecklenburg County Multi-Jurisdictional Hazard Mitigation Plan (2005)

- General Development Policies (2007)

- Centers, Corridors and Wedges Growth Framework (2008–draft)

- Mecklenburg County Parks & Recreation Greenway Plan (2008–update)

In addition, the following experts reviewed the case study to ensure accuracy:

- David Canaan, Director, Mecklenburg County Land and Water Resources

- Julie Clark, Division Director, Greenway Planning and Development

- Garet Johnson, Assistant Director, Long Range Planning Services and Strategic Planning Services

- Gavin Smith, Executive Director, Center for the Study of Natural Hazards and Disasters at the University of North Carolina–Chapel Hill

- Tim Trautman, Program Manager, Mecklenburg County Flood Mitigation

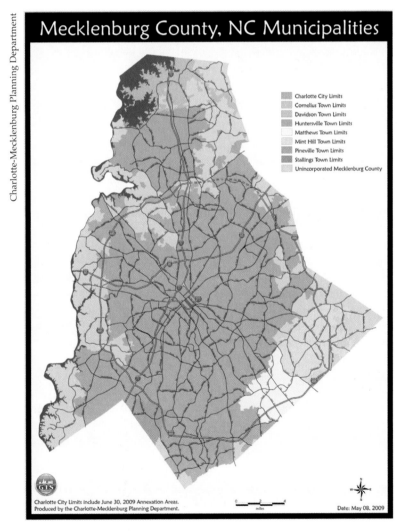

Figure 6.8. *Map of Mecklenburg County*

Purpose and Method

The purpose of this case study is to explore how Charlotte-Mecklenburg staff successfully developed hazard mitigation planning and integrated those strategies into local planning activities. Charlotte-Mecklenburg was one of the earliest communities in the United States to quantify and map flood elevations and floodplain boundaries based on "future land-use" conditions. Thus, Charlotte-Mecklenburg is a model of how to anticipate and measure impacts of natural hazards based on future development. Early in the modeling process, Charlotte-Mecklenburg staff secured buy-in for its future floodplain remapping program among stakeholders (property owners and developers) and elected officials. Therefore, Charlotte-Mecklenburg is a model of outreach and communicative participation. Finally, Charlotte-Mecklenburg staff successfully integrated the future floodplain remapping program together with a water-quality protection program and parks and recreation planning, but integration with area planning and other policy-guidance documents was weak. Thus, Charlotte-Mecklenburg is a model of how to integrate hazard mitigation planning with other local planning activities through strong interdepartmental cooperation and collaborative implementation, and it demonstrates as well how there is room for improvement to involve planning staff more proactively in the hazard mitigation planning process. This case study will examine both the strengths and opportunities for enhancement with Charlotte-Mecklenburg's approach.

The State of North Carolina reached a major turning point in its approach to hazard mitigation planning in 1996, immediately following hurricanes Bertha and Fran. In response to the impacts of those two disasters, the state Division of Emergency Management launched the Hazard Mitigation Planning Initiative (HMPI) (NCEMD 2000). The ultimate goal of the HMPI was to reduce community vulnerability to natural hazards through mitigation policy and projects. This goal would be met by integrating hazard mitigation principles into the day-to-day decision making of local governments. Mecklenburg County was selected as one of 11 Demonstration Communities to develop local hazard mitigation plans in coordination with state-level guidelines. The development of watershed-based hazard mitigation plans led to the identification of flood-prone properties that were ultimately targeted for acquisition and relocation using FEMA Hazard Mitigation Grant Program funds and other state program funding that became widely available following hurricanes Bertha, Fran, and, later in 1999, Floyd.

In 1999, Mecklenburg County was also selected as one of FEMA's Project Impact communities. Project Impact aimed to create "disaster-resistant" communities through public-private collaborations to form local partnerships, assess risk, implement risk-reduction actions, and communicate success. HMPI and Project Impact positioned Charlotte-Mecklenburg to launch its own hazard mitigation initiative to address those problem areas that became evident following severe flood events in 1995 and 1997.

Background: Hazards, Geography, and Institutions

A community's natural hazards, geographic setting, and regulatory environment establish the context for both hazard mitigation planning and integration of hazard mitigation into other local planning. Charlotte-Mecklenburg faces significant natural hazards, primarily flooding and severe weather including tropical storms, with increasing vulnerability due to rapid growth and development. In response, Charlotte-Mecklenburg staff has established collaborative networks among agencies, stakeholders, and elected officials. Innovative programs were developed to mitigate hazard impacts through floodplain remapping, stakeholder outreach, and integration with water-quality programs, area plans, and recreational greenways.

According to the Mecklenburg Multi-Jurisdictional Hazard Mitigation Plan (2005), the vulnerability analysis shows that property worth approximately $99.3 billion is exposed to hazard impacts. The top five natural hazards, ranked by estimated annualized property loss (Table 6.2), are: hurricanes and tropical storms ($4.5 million); earthquakes ($1.8 million); floods ($1.2 million); drought ($0.7 million); and winter storms ($0.3 million). The analysis also includes a Priority Risk Index of hazards based on a qualitative assessment of each hazard's probability, impact, spatial extent, warning time, and duration: (1) flood; (2) hurricanes and tropical storms; (3) winter storms; (4) severe thunderstorms; and (5) tornadoes. A combination of the quantitative and qualitative assessments and the general consensus of the Mitigation Planning Committee identified the same five hazards as high risk for Mecklenburg County. Earthquakes, drought, and wildfire were categorized as moderate risks. (See Table 6.3.)

TABLE 6.2. COMPARISON OF ANNUALIZED LOSS ESTIMATES AND PRIORITY RISK INDEX VALUES

QUANTITATIVE ASSESSMENT FINDINGS		QUALITATIVE ASSESSMENT FINDINGS	
HAZARD	ANNUALIZED LOSS ESTIMATES	HAZARD	PRI VALUE
Hurricanes and Tropical Storms	$4,544,000	Flood	3.3
Earthquakes	$1,775,000	Winter Storms	3.0
Flood	$1,154,000	Hurricanes and Tropical Storms	2.9
Drought	$656,805	Severe Thunderstorms	2.7
Winter Storms	$283,383	Tornadoes	2.7
Severe Thunderstorms	$127,119	Drought	2.6
Tornadoes	$81,821	Earthquakes	2.6
Wildfire	$9,017	Wildfire	2.6
Dam/Levee Failure	Negligible	Dam/Levee Failure	2.3
Sinkholes	Negligible	Sinkholes	2.0
Landslides	Negligible	Landslides	1.4

Source: Mecklenburg County Multi-Jurisdictional Hazard Mitigation Plan

TABLE 6.3. CONCLUSIONS ON HAZARD RISK FOR MECKLENBURG COUNTY

High Risk	Hurricanes and Tropical Storms Flood Winter Storms Severe Thunderstorms Tornadoes
Moderate Risk	Earthquakes Drought Wildfire
Low Risk	Dam/Levee Failure Sinkholes Landslides

Source: Mecklenburg County Multi-Jurisdictional Hazard Mitigation Plan

Mecklenburg County's rapid growth has increased its vulnerability to natural hazards, particularly flood hazards. Between 1984 and 2001, Mecklenburg County lost more than 22 percent of its tree cover and 22 percent of its open space. Over that same period, the county's impervious surface area increased by 127 percent (American Forests 2003), as the natural environment was replaced by parking lots, rooftops, streets, and buildings. This has reduced stormwater retention capacity and exacerbated the impacts of flooding rainfall from hurricanes, tropical storms, and severe thunderstorms.

Section 322 of the Disaster Mitigation Act of 2000 requires that state and local governments develop a hazard mitigation plan to remain eligible for pre- and postdisaster mitigation funding. Mecklenburg County utilized the multijurisdictional planning process recommended by FEMA (Publication Series 386) to develop its plan, which was prepared in coordination with the North Carolina Emergency Management Division (NCEMD) and published in 2005. Shortly thereafter, the plan was approved by FEMA and adopted by each of the participating jurisdictions; it is monitored and updated on a routine basis to maintain compliance with both federal legislation and the North Carolina General Statutes.[1] The 2010 update to the hazard mitigation plan will be developed by the Charlotte-Mecklenburg Emergency Management Office (CMEMO), which also maintains the All Hazards Plan for Mecklenburg County jurisdictions.

Prior to the DMA, the State of North Carolina established a framework for hazard mitigation planning by characterizing responses to natural hazards as a critical dimension of urban and regional sustainability. The 1999 Governor's Interagency Quality Growth Task Force inventoried the roles and impacts of state programs on land use, development patterns, and exposure to natural hazards (NCEMD 2000). Following Hurricane Floyd in 1999, NCEMD encouraged redevelopment through a set of guiding principles modeled after goals established in 1996 by President Clinton's Council on Sustainable Development: economic prosperity, social equity, natural-area conservation, affordable and safe housing, and natural-hazard risk reduction. The Department of City and Regional Planning (DCRP) at the University of North Carolina was tapped for its expertise in sustainable development and hazard mitigation. David Godschalk and colleagues advanced four principles to guide short-term recovery and redevelopment in a 1999 letter to the governor (NCEMD 2000):

- Relocate or protect critical facilities located within floodplains

- Buy out and relocate vulnerable homes and businesses

- Relocate and prohibit unsafe land-use activities

- Maintain and restore the natural mitigation functions of floodplains

The DCRP also prepared three planning guidebooks to support the Hazard Mitigation Planning Initiative: (1) an overview of the mitigation planning process; (2) a step-by-step planning workbook for smaller and rural jurisdictions; and (3) a "tools and techniques" compendium for local governments.

Charlotte-Mecklenburg Storm Water Services embraced the policies outlined by NCEMD as key anchors of its initiatives to mitigate the impacts of flooding and improve water quality in Mecklenburg County. It employs a full-time staff of 153 and has an annual budget of $73.8 million (2008–2009), supported in part by a Storm Water Fee.[2] Its responsibilities include preventing or reducing the loss of life, disruption of services, and property damage caused by floods; providing a quality storm-drainage system that is safe, clean, and cost-effective; mapping floodplains and managing floodplain development; preserving and restoring natural stream channels and the beneficial functions of floodplains; monitoring pollutant levels in surface water; investigating spills or illegal dumping; enforcing ordinances designed to protect water quality; educating residents about pollution prevention; and restoring the paths and banks of eroded or damaged streams.

The primary planning agency is the Charlotte-Mecklenburg Planning Department, although each of the six towns in the county has its own planning department. There are two primary divisions within the planning department: Development Services and Long Range Planning and Strategic Planning Services. The department develops general plans and policy documents, district plans, and area plans; coordinates rezoning and approves subdivision and multifamily-residential development plans; provides information and research assistance to the public and other agencies; coordinates transportation and transit planning with land-use planning and supports the Mecklenburg Union Metropolitan Planning Organization (MUMPO); assesses the need for capital improvements in terms of adopted plans; coordinates the annexation process; and assists with area economic-development efforts through corridor revitalization planning, research, and demographic data analysis.

Charlotte-Mecklenburg Flood Hazard Mitigation Planning

Future Land Use Map (FLUM) and Future Floodplain Initiative. In the 1970s, FEMA developed 100-year floodplain boundary maps to illustrate which areas would be inundated during a rainfall event with a 1 percent annual chance of occurrence. Such maps depicted the flood elevations and floodplain boundaries based on current land use. This practice remains the standard for FEMA floodplain mapping throughout the United States under the NFIP and its new Risk MAP program.[3] However, FEMA did not update floodplain maps regularly to reflect the increase in flood elevations and spatial area covered by the 100-year flood caused by increased runoff from new development. In an area that experiences dynamic growth and development, as Charlotte-Mecklenburg has, significant change to flood elevations and floodplain boundaries may occur within a single year. The disjunction between predicted and actual floodplains due to outdated maps motivated the development of Charlotte-Mecklenburg's Floodplain Land Use Map (FLUM) and Future Floodplain Initiative.[4]

The most severe flood events in Mecklenburg County occurred in August 1995 and July 1997 (MCEM 2005). In August 1995, the remnants of Tropical Storm Jerry dumped four to 10 inches of rain across the region. Approximately $4 million in flood insurance claims from 250 buildings were paid, and $1 million in loans were issued to fund repairs. In July 1997, rainfall from Hurricane Danny peaked at more than 13 inches. Danny caused $8.5 million in property damage in Mecklenburg County, and flood insurance claims were paid on 400 buildings. Danny's floodwaters killed three people, including a girl in Charlotte who was swept into a creek.

In both cases, significant flooding occurred in areas outside the FEMA-mapped 100-year floodplain. Charlotte-Mecklenburg Storm Water Services staff realized that the actual floodplains had expanded beyond the boundaries marked in FEMA's 1975 Flood Insurance Study. Their initial solution was to model and map new floodplain boundaries based on 1995 land cover. However, officials quickly realized that these maps would also quickly become obsolete because of rapid growth and development, and so they sought to capture the maximum possible extent of any future 100-year flood event by modeling flood elevations and floodplain boundaries based on "build-out land-use" conditions, using the current zoning ordinance and future land-use and population growth projections. This Future Land Use Map and Future Floodplain Initiative was outlined in the Mecklenburg County Floodplain Guidance Management Document (Charlotte-Mecklenburg Storm Water Services 1997)

The Mecklenburg County Floodplain Management Guidance Document was formally adopted in December 1997. A symposium on floodplains introduced the remapping program to the public in 1998 with pilot studies of Mallard and McAlpine creeks. In 1999, Charlotte-Mecklenburg filed applications for Hazard Mitigation Grant Program (HMGP) funds to help support the remapping effort.[5] The application development and submittal were dramatically expedited by the detailed information the county had already compiled about its flood-prone homes. In addition to FEMA funds, remapping support came from the U.S. Army Corps of Engineers and Charlotte-Mecklenburg stormwater utility fees. By August 2002, the 16 major watersheds of Mecklenburg County had been remapped at a cost of $3 million. The new maps received FEMA approval in February 2004.

There are now two floodplain boundaries mapped for Charlotte-Mecklenburg: the FEMA floodplain boundary (updated to 1998 land use) and the future (or community) floodplain boundary. (See Figure 6.9. The FEMA floodplain is shown in light blue; the future floodplain is in gray.) Property owners in a FEMA-regulated floodplain must have flood insurance, while flood insurance is strongly recommended but not required in the future floodplain. The City of Charlotte, Mecklenburg County, and the six towns have floodplain development ordinances that place additional restrictions on building or renovations in both floodplains.

Stakeholder Participation and Outreach. Charlotte-Mecklenburg officials faced a major policy dilemma that required careful resolution to ensure a successful floodplain-remapping program. Delineating floodplains based on the future-conditions modeling initiative meant a significantly greater area would be classified as either a flood risk or contributing to flood risk and would be subject to more stringent regulation. Removing or limiting potential development opportunities was antithetical to Charlotte-Mecklenburg's tradition of welcoming growth. Recognizing this, a broad-based collection of interests—including developers, environmentalists, representatives of community organizations, planners, engineers, county commissioners, and city officials and their staffs—was brought to the table to craft an acceptable solution.

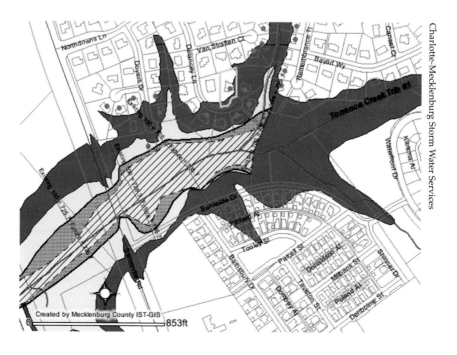

Figure 6.9. *FEMA and future floodplain boundaries within an area of Charlotte-Mecklenburg*

Charlotte-Mecklenburg Storm Water Services

Developers, stakeholders, and elected officials had to recognize the flood hazard problem for themselves if they were to embrace the initiative. Although area developers seemed to understand the normative objectives of Charlotte-Mecklenburg Storm Water Services to protect life and property, they were not inclined to yield property. Storm Water Services responded with pilot studies and model runs of Mallard Creek and McAlpine Creek that showed significant differences between the FEMA and FLUM approaches in calculating floodplain coverage and flood heights. Although negotiations, discussions, and exchanges lasted for about three years, the model output data from the pilot watersheds and continuing education by Storm Water Services convinced the Real Estate Board of Commissioners (REBC) and the Chamber of Commerce to endorse the initiative. Their endorsement and the encouragement of others led the development community to believe that remapped floodplains would undergird regulations based on "good science." Some respected civil engineers reviewed the modeling methods on behalf of their developer clients and convinced the development community that the government officials and consultants were doing sound work (Trautman 2009).

Charlotte-Mecklenburg Storm Water Services also built support through model transparency and interactive data sharing. For example, they illustrated a number of scenarios demonstrating how flood elevations change given different floodplain build-out scenarios—elevations increased by as much as 11 feet—and how the floodway expands.[6] Anticipated flood losses were quantified under these conditions. Because Storm Water Services tied proposed actions or inaction to real dollar figures, developers and county commissioners took notice. Another example is the Floodzone Interactive Map, which is available online and allows citizens to create their own depictions of floodplain maps based on specific geographic input.[7] When maps were being unveiled in 2001 and 2002, there was no severe backlash, and the maps were adopted without significant uproar. The Floodzone Interactive Map has raised awareness among property owners that the floodplain is expanding. Although some property owners do not like the prospect of expanded regulation based on something that might happen in the future, they do appreciate direct access to the information driving policy.

Integration of Flood Hazard Mitigation with Water Quality Planning

Charlotte-Mecklenburg staff successfully integrated the future-floodplain remapping program with a water-quality protection program. The Surface Water Improvement and Management (SWIM) Program was established by the Mecklenburg County Department of Environmental Protection in November 1995. Although the SWIM initiative began as a drive for improved water quality, its timing allowed for a synergistic relationship with the FLUM initiative. The land-use and development policies that relate to floodplain management translated to SWIM policies to protect water quality through flood hazard mitigation.

Through SWIM, Mecklenburg County commissioners established a goal of improving water quality to a level that would allow for "prolonged human contact." A coalition of environmentalists, citizens, developers, and local officials created a stream buffer plan that defined buffer widths based on the acreage drained by each creek or stream. The larger the drainage area, the larger the buffer required. If the buffer area exceeded the mapped floodplain, new development was not allowed within the buffer, even though it was outside the floodplain. By keeping the buffer free of development, the existing vegetation filtered pollutants, while the open space provided for additional water storage.

Since 1999, significant regulatory progress has been made in redirecting how developers build in Mecklenburg County. In 2004, the Low-Impact Development Ordinance was developed in partnership with Charlotte-Mecklenburg Storm Water Services and passed in Huntersville, one of the six towns within the county. Huntersville was considered a good pilot for this ordinance because most of the town lies within the McDowell Creek Watershed, whose outlet into Lake Norman sits just upstream from a major water-supply intake for Charlotte-Mecklenburg. In June 2007, Mecklenburg County and the six towns each adopted a Post-Construction Storm Water Ordinance. Federal law requires the adoption of such ordinances as part of permits mandated by the Clean Water Act under terms of the county and towns' Joint Phase II Storm Water Permit. The purpose is to control storm-water pollutants as well as the volume and flow of stormwater runoff from new development and redevelopment.[8] Overall goals of a postconstruction stormwater ordinance include:

- Complying with state and federal regulations

- Minimizing pollution in streams and lakes

- Reducing stream-bank erosion and flood risks

- Preserving undisturbed stream buffers and open space

- Protecting endangered aquatic species

- Reducing long-term costs for watershed restoration

Integration of Flood Hazard Mitigation with Community Planning

The Buyout Program. Charlotte-Mecklenburg Storm Water Services established its Floodplain Buyout Program as part of its hazard-mitigation planning process, which included its floodplain remapping initiative. Property owners could sell their homes and businesses to the county if their property was a repeat victim of flooding. The purpose of the buyout program was to (1) protect the lives of residents who had already suffered impacts of flooding by giving them an opportunity to move out of high-risk flood zones, and to (2) remove development from the future floodplain to allow the floodplain to revert to natural vegetation growth and redevelop its functions of flood mitigation and water-quality protection.

In 1999, Storm Water Services applied for HMGP funds to help pay for the cost of the voluntary buyout program (known as "Hurricane Fran Grants"). Financial support was 75 percent federal ($48 million) and 25 percent state ($10 million) and local ($6 million). Local funds came from the Charlotte-Mecklenburg Storm Water Utility Fee, begun in 1993. By 2009, about 225 properties (210 single- and multifamily residential; 15 commercial) had been purchased (Trautman 2009). The county applied total demolition to purchased structures; there was no physical relocation of buildings. Owners of single-family homes who volunteered for the buyout program found another dwelling on their own. Renters of single-family homes or residents of multifamily dwellings were offered relocation assistance. Similar arrangements were made for commercial buyout participants (business owners relocated on their own; commercial-space renters were offered relocation assistance).

Parks and Recreation Planning. The 2008 update of the Mecklenburg County Greenway Master Plan exemplifies how flood hazard mitigation has been successfully integrated into Parks and Recreation Department objectives to work with other county agencies, improve efficiency of network trail development, and concentrate more on stream corridor and floodplain protection. When the Floodplain Buyout Program provided an opportunity for the county to allow the future floodplain to revert to open space, the Parks and Recreation Department, working with Storm Water Services, used that newly created space to expand the Mecklenburg County Greenway and permanently protect stream buffers. This nexus between disaster resilience and sustainable development reduced flood risk, improved water quality, and provided local recreational opportunities. As of the 2008 Greenway Master Plan Update (Figure 6.10), Parks and Recreation has "designed and constructed over 30 miles of trail within 14 greenway corridors. Over 3,000 acres of floodplain and riparian habitat have been conserved. The 5 Year Action Plan calls for the construction of 43 miles of new greenway trail by 2013 and 62 miles of new greenway trail by 2018" (Mecklenburg County Department of Parks and Recreation 2008).

Area Planning. The ability to guide development in a manner that respects identified hazard areas is an important long-term aspect of hazard mitigation and should be included in a community comprehensive plan (Smith 2008). The comprehensive plan incorporates broad policy guidance regarding future growth. However, according to Garet Johnson, Director of Long Range Planning Services and Strategic Planning Services for the Charlotte-Mecklenburg Planning Department, there is no mandate for comprehensive planning in Mecklenburg County. Furthermore, Charlotte-Mecklenburg

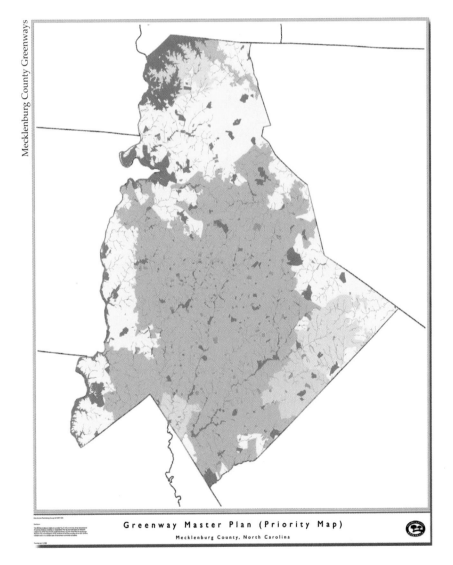

Mecklenburg County Greenways

Greenway Master Plan (Priority Map)
Mecklenburg County, North Carolina

Figure 6.10. 2008 Mecklenburg County Greenway Master Plan

planning staff had somewhat limited involvement in the development of the 2005 Mecklenburg County Multi-Jurisdictional Hazard Mitigation Plan. The result is somewhat limited integration of hazard mitigation with planning policy documents.

Charlotte-Mecklenburg has developed broad policy guidance regarding future growth through several documents: the 2015 Plan; the Centers, Corridors and Wedges Growth Framework (Charlotte-Mecklenburg Planning Department 2008); general development policies (Charlotte-Mecklenburg Planning Department 2007); and area plans. While all of these documents provide broad, general guidelines regarding environmental preservation and open space conservation, Charlotte-Mecklenburg planners specifically integrate the future floodplain boundaries into area-plan maps.

More than 60 area plans have been developed since 1991; they incorporate more detail than documents like the 2015 Plan.[9] The Charlotte-Mecklenburg Planning Department develops area plans to guide growth and development so that they occur in a manner consistent with stakeholders' visions. Area plans vary in scope, depending on the geographic area and purpose of the plan. The plans typically address land use and zoning, transportation, environment, infrastructure, economic development (including revitalization), community appearance, community safety, and urban design. Citizens are encouraged to participate in the area planning process. In some instances, the plan may also recommend rezoning as part of plan implementation.

Despite broad planning policy development in Charlotte-Mecklenburg during the last two decades, area plans (as well as the other comprehensive planning documents) do not directly address hazard mitigation policy. According to Johnson, the language used in documents such as the area plans and general development policies to "protect environmental resources" implies protection of life and property from natural-hazard threat because environmentally sensitive areas correlate with the future floodplain (labeled "open space" or "recreation area"). According to Johnson, direct references are not employed because of concerns about private property rights and perceived takings. Another possible explanation may be that only one staff member from Development Services—and none from Long Range Planning and Strategic Planning Services—participated in the development of the 2005 Mecklenburg County Multi-Jurisdictional Hazard Mitigation Plan. Upon review of the draft plan, that staff member felt that the connection between the environment and land use was not adequately addressed; the focus was mainly on emergency management.

Lessons Learned

Charlotte-Mecklenburg was one of the earliest communities in the United States to quantify and map flood elevations and floodplain boundaries based on "build-out land-use" conditions. It is a vanguard community in the effort to mitigate the impacts of flooding by educating, involving, and assisting constituents in reshaping settlement patterns to avoid high-risk flood zones. Through the initiative of the Storm Water Services staff, Charlotte-Mecklenburg blazed a trail for other communities not only to mitigate current hazards but to anticipate and mitigate potential impacts of natural hazards based on future development.

Charlotte-Mecklenburg staff secured buy-in for its future floodplain remapping program among stakeholders and elected officials. Storm Water Services provided transparent methods, understandable data, and interactive mapping to educate property owners, developers, and elected officials about what build-out of the zoning code would lead to in future flooding events. Stakeholders embraced the openness exhibited by Storm Water Services. The maps made sense, and the dollar estimates of potential property loss hit home. Charlotte-Mecklenburg demonstrated how proactive outreach and communicative participation can achieve tangible results.

Charlotte-Mecklenburg found mixed success in integrating flood hazard mitigation into other planning activities and community objectives. Water-quality protection and parks and recreation planning are models of successful integration. However, the current approach is largely reactionary—planners decide where new development will occur, flood maps get revised to reflect the impacts on flood elevations and boundaries, and then restrictions are imposed as a result of the boundary expansion. Charlotte-Mecklenburg Storm Water Services, Emergency Management, and Planning staff members need to come together more deliberately. The thread of hazard mitigation is somewhat weak in the long-term and strategic planning policy documents that guide the vision for the region. Planners have not been at the table to discuss and guide broader hazard mitigation policy. As a result, references to hazards are few to nonexistent in policy documents, and similarly scarce are references to land-use planning in hazard mitigation documents. A more proactive approach to integrate hazard mitigation and planning would be for planners to simulate the effects of alternative future land scenarios on floodplain boundaries.

As successful as Charlotte-Mecklenburg Storm Water Services has been, it needs to bring more planners into the hazard mitigation fold. The 2010 Mecklenburg County Multi-Jurisdictional Hazard Mitigation Plan Update is a timely opportunity.

NOTES

1. Chapter 166A: North Carolina Emergency Management Act, as amended by Senate Bill 300: An Act to Amend the Laws Regarding Emergency Management as Recommended by the Legislative Disaster Response and Recovery Commission (2001).

2. The fee pays for stormwater programs in Mecklenburg County and the seven municipalities. A portion of all Charlotte-Mecklenburg stormwater revenue goes to countywide efforts to reduce flood risks, improve water quality, and restore streams. This is called the "major system" fee. Generally speaking, the county administers stormwater programs involving named streams and regulated floodplains. Drainage systems inside Charlotte and the six towns are part of the "minor system." This system includes channels, pipes, storm drains, and culverts on private property and in the street rights-of-way. For each county stormwater-fee dollar spent on flood mitigation, Mecklenburg County receives as much as three dollars in federal and state grants. For each such dollar spent on water quality, Mecklenburg County receives nearly two dollars in federal and state grants. See www.charmeck.org/Departments/StormWater/Storm+Water+Fee/Where+does+the+money+go%3f.htm.

3. Risk MAP also includes more attention to risk assessment and planning, as well as risk communication, compared to the traditional NFIP.

4. Since the FEMA floodplain maps drive insurance decisions, development decisions, public policy, and emergency management, disjunction between the predicted and actual floods may mean unanticipated costs and threats to life and property.

5. Since federal funds for remapping were made available under Map Modernization, now RiskMAP, FEMA's HMGP no longer funds flood studies.

6. A "regulatory floodway" is the channel of a river or other watercourse and the adjacent land areas that must be reserved in order to discharge the base flood without cumulatively increasing the water surface elevation more than a designated height. Communities must regulate

development in these floodways to ensure that there are no increases in upstream flood elevations. For streams and other watercourses where FEMA has provided Base Flood Elevations (BFEs) but no floodway has been designated, the community must review floodplain development on a case-by-case basis to ensure that increases in water surface elevations do not occur, or they must identify the need to designate a floodway if adequate information is available. See www.fema.gov/plan/prevent/floodplain/nfipkeywords/floodway.shtm.

7. See http://maps.co.mecklenburg.nc.us/website/floodzone.

8. The Standards Section (Section 3) of the Post-Construction Storm Water Ordinance describes the specific criteria that all applicable development and redevelopment must meet in order to control water quality, volume, and velocity as required by the ordinance:

  1. Installation of structural best management practices (BMPs) when a built-upon area threshold is exceeded.
  2. Maintenance of buffers (no-build zones) adjacent to perennial and intermittent streams.
  3. Installation of detention measures when a built-upon area threshold is exceeded.

In addition, new developments in all the jurisdictions except the towns of Cornelius and Huntersville are required to set aside undisturbed open space as a form of nonstructural BMP. This criterion does not apply to redevelopment. Huntersville has open space requirements outside of the Post-Construction Storm Water Ordinance (Charlotte-Mecklenburg County Storm Water Services 2007, p. 13).

9. The 2015 Plan is not a land-use plan. The 2005 Plan and each of the Planning Commission's seven district plans (Central, Northeast, Northwest, South, Southwest, East, and North) provide the land-use policy direction for Charlotte-Mecklenburg. The 2015 Plan does not provide this level of detail. The 2015 Plan is a policy document that establishes a number of priority areas that city and county government and the greater community should focus on to ensure that Charlotte-Mecklenburg remains economically viable and continues to offer a high quality of life in the next century. See www.charmeck.org/Departments/Planning/Area+Planning/Plans/2015+Plan/Home.htm.

CHAPTER 7

Case Studies: Intermediate Jurisdictions

ROSEVILLE, CALIFORNIA
Kenneth C. Topping, FAICP

Roseville, a rapidly expanding suburb of Sacramento, California, features the largest rail yard west of the Mississippi River and seven creeks that feed into one drainage basin. Disasters in Roseville have included a major explosion at the rail yard in 1973 and several major flood events. Home to high-tech and health-care industries, the community has taken a proactive approach to protecting its growing asset base, leveraging flood-hazard mitigation actions within a comprehensive planning framework, and using a vigorous economic development program as an engine for creating sustainability.

Mitigation of natural and human-caused hazards is an essential part of the community's state-mandated general plan, as well as its federally guided Local Hazard Mitigation Plan, prepared under the Disaster Mitigation Act of 2000. Roseville actively engages stakeholders in the monitoring of plan progress, and it has used the Community Rating System, its general plan, and the Roseville Hazard Mitigation Plan as foundations for promoting long-term economic and disaster resilience.

This case study focuses on the following documents:

- California Governor's Office of Planning and Research, *General Plan Guidelines* (2003)

- California Governor's Office of Emergency Services, 2007 State of California Multi-Hazard Mitigation Plan

- Brian Laughlin, "Roseville Flood Mitigation," unpublished paper (June 2009)

- Roseville 2020 General Plan Safety Element (2003)

- Roseville Hazard Mitigation Plan (June 2005)

In addition, interviews were conducted with the following people:

- Julia Burrows, Deputy City Manager, City of Roseville

- Robert Flaner, Senior Planner, Tetra Tech

- Rhon Herndon, Engineering Manager, City of Roseville

- Paul Richardson, Planning Director, City of Roseville

Setting and Population

Roseville is 20 miles east of Sacramento, near the base of the foothills of the Sierra Nevada range. Established during the mid-19th-century gold rush, the community grew rapidly in the early 1900s with establishment of a rail roundhouse and repair and yard facilities. It became an incorporated city in 1909. By the 1920s, Roseville had the largest freight yard west of the Mississippi River. Growth spurts after World War II substantially increased the community's population. The arrival of the high-tech firms Hewlett-Packard and NEC during the 1980s spurred economic development. Since 1990, the city's population has more than tripled, and in the past decade the U.S. Census identified Roseville as the sixth-fastest-growing city in the country.

Roseville had an estimated population of 112,000 in 2009 and is the largest city in Placer County, with a third of the county's population. Along with El Dorado, Sacramento, and Yolo counties, Placer County is part of the Sacramento Metropolitan Area, which borders on the Sacramento–San Joaquin Delta region and has a history of flooding.

Disaster Experience

The Roseville Hazard Mitigation Plan (RHMP) ranks human-caused events as a top hazard because of a major explosion and chemical-plume release in the rail yards in April 1973, when 6,000 bombs on a train bound for the Concord Naval Weapons Station detonated after a car caught fire (Figure 7.2). The blast injured more than 350 people and damaged 5,500 buildings, some more than a mile away.

Although the explosion was dramatic, flooding later matched it as a hazard of major concern. Roseville is divided by two drainage basins (Figure 7.3).

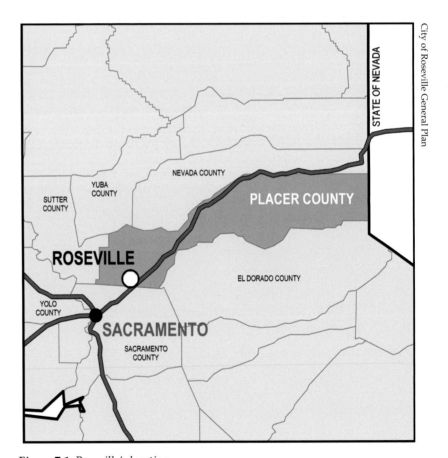

Figure 7.1. Roseville's location

Figure 7.2. *Three views of the 1973 Roseville rail yard explosion*

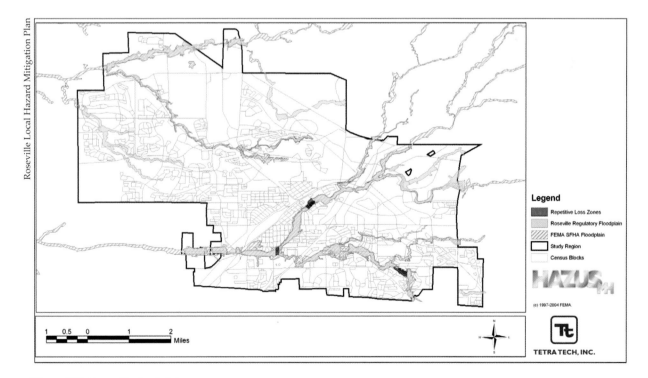

Figure 7.3. *Roseville floodplains*

The Pleasant Grove Creek Basin, which crosses the northwestern end of the city, has intermittent seasonal stream flows and no structures within its 100-year floodplain. Since 1950, no structural damage from flooding has occurred. By contrast, the Dry Creek Basin, which crosses the southeastern end, has a year-round flow. Between 1950 and 2003, 10 major floods resulted in more than $37 million in property damage, with the worst floods occurring in 1983, 1986, and 1995 (Laughlin 2009). Damages were incurred in older subdivisions that were built in the 1960s and 1970s, when floodplain mapping was not as accurate as it is today.

Learning from Disasters

After these events, the community mobilized action to prevent future flood losses. For example, after the 1983 flood damaged 25 homes, six businesses, and two bridges, the California Legislature created the Placer County Flood Control and Water Conservation District, with a nine-member governing board comprising city and county representatives. The district generated the Dry Creek Watershed Flood Control Plan, which includes regional detention basins and other improvements for which developer fees have been collected. In 1985, the city contracted with an engineering firm to undertake a hydrological analysis leading to the 1986 publication of a Future Floodplain Map that showed the 100-year floodplain based on future land-use conditions and projected growth, not on existing conditions. The community then used this regulatory map, which showed a 100-year floodplain area greater than that on the FIRM maps, in restricting development within the floodplain's perimeters. Although never formally adopted, the study has been used by the city as the best available information for regulatory and land-use programs such as specific plans and improvement standards.

As a result of the 1986 flood, the city's improvement standards were revised to require all new developments to have an "overland release," to be used in the event of a completely plugged underground storm-drain system. The combination of the 1986 mapping and this requirement has virtually eliminated the flood threat for development projects constructed since then; no structures constructed in Roseville since the mid-1980s have experienced flooding. However, Roseville has older areas that are still at risk of flooding.

The 1995 flood was much larger than the 1986 flood, damaging 358 structures valued at $4.4 million and causing $8 million total damage (Figure 7.4). This flood generated substantial public interest in taking aggressive action, as well as a visit by President Bill Clinton, and led to appropriation of federal funds to construct flood control improvements, elevate homes above base flood elevations, and buy out flood-prone properties. Since the 1995 flood, more than $20 million in flood control improvements have been implemented in Roseville.

Responses under NFIP and CRS

Roseville began participating in the National Flood Insurance Program (NFIP) in 1983, and joined the Community Rating System (CRS) in 1991. NFIP requires participants to follow two basic criteria: All new buildings and developments undergoing major improvements must be elevated to or above the 100-year flood level, and new developments within portions of the floodplain must not increase flood problems or damage other properties.

From 1986 through 2001, Roseville expended $12.8 million in city funds on flood protection, home elevation, and land-acquisition projects, and it achieved a federal match from FEMA of $11.2 million for such projects (Table 7.1). More important, it saved many more dollars in future flood losses. For each dollar spent by the city on hazardous-property acquisition activity alone during this period, eight dollars' worth of flood losses have been avoided

Figure 7.4. View of the 1995 floods in Roseville

TABLE 7.1. EXAMPLES OF FLOOD IMPROVEMENTS FROM 1986 TO 2001

Year	Project	Approx. Cost
1986	Quadrupled size of culvert at Rocky Ridge Drive on Linda Creek to handle 100-year storm	$250,000
1986	Added culvert at Champion Oaks Drive at Linda Creek and improved channel upstream to increase channel capacity	$100,000
1986	Improved culvert at Union Pacific tracks on Dry Creek	$100,000
1990	Enlarged culvert under Diamond Oaks Road, thereby protecting 10 homes that flooded in 1986	$250,000
1992	Replaced Loretto Bridge over Cirby Creek and widened channel between Eich School and Sierra Gardens Drive, bringing all nearby homes out of floodplain	$700,000
1993	Replaced Diamond Oaks culvert, bringing all nearby homes out of floodplain	$500,000
1996	Removed culvert under Union Pacific railroad tracks on Dry Creek downstream of Vernon Street, removing more than 150 homes from the floodplain, lowering flood elevations by 5 to 7 feet	$2 million (city portion $220,000)
1996	Cirby Creek/I-80 project (Tina/Elisa area) included channel excavation and construction of berms and floodwalls. Brought entire Tina/Elisa neighborhood of 40 homes out of floodplain through acquisition. Entire area would have flooded during a 1997 flood if improvements and acquisitions had not occurred	$3 million (100% city funded)
2001	Elevated structures not completely brought out of the floodplain by flood-control project construction. With voluntary home owner participation, 27 of 44 homes elevated, most located in Folsom/Maciel neighborhood along Dry Creek	$1 million (75% FEMA funded)
2001	Flood-control improvements on Linda Creek in the Champion Oaks/West Colonial Parkway and Sunrise/Oakridge areas replaced culverts with a bridge. Floodwalls and channel excavation brought 233 homes out of floodplain and reduced risk to 44 additional homes. Channel maintained in near natural state, with planting of more than 500 oaks	$16.1 million ($8.7 million from FEMA, $7.4 million in city funds)

Source: City of Roseville Flood Facts

(Burrows 2009). Additionally, in the time since floodwalls were constructed along Dry Creek with the support of FEMA Hazard Mitigation Grant Program (HMPG) funds, no losses have occurred there (Figure 7.5).

As a result of its proactive floodplain management program, Roseville by 2002 had achieved a CRS Class 5 rating. (See sidebar, p. 17.) In 2006, it became the first community in the country to earn a Class 1 rating, resulting in 45 percent discounts of flood insurance for policy holders (Roseville 2005a).

Role of the Comprehensive Plan

Prior to adoption of the RHMP, flood hazard mitigation was carried out within a comprehensive policy framework established by the city's general plan. The Roseville general plan was adopted as a comprehensive plan in 1972 and revised extensively in 1992. The general plan safety element was an important factor in determining flood hazard mitigation policy for the community, essentially setting the stage for much of the city's flood mitigation actions during the late 1990s.

California does not have a statewide growth-management system such as those in Washington and Florida. California laws instead emphasize local accountability for coordinated local planning and implementation actions, which must meet broad state standards. These laws include requirements for a comprehensive general plan with which zoning, subdivision, and local development permitting decisions must be consistent. At the center of these laws is the requirement that all cities and counties prepare and adopt a general plan as a comprehensive statement of future development goals, policies, and planned implementation actions. All general plans must include seven elements—land use, circulation, housing, safety, conservation, open space, and noise—which in turn must be consistent with one another. The safety element must reflect local hazards together with plans for their reduction. Most fundamentally, implementation actions—including zoning, subdivisions, capital improvements, and permits—must all be consistent with the general plan.

Figure 7.5. A Roseville floodwall

Roseville Hazard Mitigation Plan

With the passage of the Disaster Mitigation Act of 2000 (DMA 2000), localities across the country were encouraged to prepare Local Hazard Mitigation Plans (LHMPs) as a necessary precondition to receiving HMGP funds under the Stafford Act. Preparation of the RHMP was initiated in 2003, and it was adopted in 2005 following an extensive public review process. It identified the following plan objectives:

- To meet or exceed DMA program requirements

- To meet both state and federal requirements as well as the needs of the city, so as to address human-caused hazards not mandated by DMA

- To provide content prescribed under CRS so Roseville could meet CRS classification prerequisites

- To coordinate existing ongoing plans and programs so that high-priority initiatives and projects to mitigate possible disaster impacts would be funded and implemented

- To create links between the RHMP and established plans, such as the city's general and specific plans, so that they can work together in achieving successful mitigation.

The RHMP served not only DMA requirements but also the needs and character of Roseville, which has a long-standing tradition of proactive, progressive planning and program implementation. This is evident in the wide variety of hazards identified in the plan's ambitious mitigation strategy, some aspects of which have already been implemented.

Linkage to the General Plan

The RHMP is a comprehensive, detailed document that integrates the policies in the city's general plan safety element and CRS objectives into a more focused mitigation planning and action framework. The plan brought a level of discipline to the city's general plan safety element in that DMA standards exceed California safety-element requirements in certain ways—for example, calling for:

1. Greater rigor in hazard and risk assessments

2. Mandatory consideration of vulnerable populations

3. Prioritization of actions as part of the mandatory hazard mitigation strategy.

The RHMP has been noted for its extraordinary thoroughness and exceptional quality, as it systematically covers natural and human-caused hazards, ranks hazards in importance, and creates a list of 71 prioritized mitigation actions linked to various ongoing city programs. An independent evaluation of the more than 400 local hazard mitigation plans approved by FEMA Region IX found the RHMP among the top 10 (Boswell et al. 2008).

Not unlike other local hazard-mitigation plans, the RHMP has expanded the scope of the general plan safety element by adding more detailed hazard, risk, and vulnerability assessments, ranking hazards and risks, and providing a detailed action plan for implementation. When finished in 2005, it was adopted jointly with the general plan safety element, so that the documents reinforce each other as foundations for community safety (Roseville 2005a and Roseville 2005b).

The RHMP and the general plan safety element are intertwined in several ways. The RHMP cites the linkage to the general plan thus:

The general plan is viewed as an integral part of the RHMP. These two planning documents will work together in their respective arenas to achieve a common goal of hazard risk reduction. Many of the action items identified in Part 4 of this RHMP are policies implemented as recommendations of the general plan. The maintenance strategy identified in Part 5 of this RHMP identifies a plan update trigger for the RHMP tied to an update of the general plan.

In January 2009, Roseville adopted the RHMP by reference as part of the safety element of its general plan under the provisions of Assembly Bill 2140, a 2006 legislative action authorizing postdisaster state financial assistance to localities jointly adopting their LHMPs and safety elements. The Roseville City Council took additional action in September 2009 to clarify references between the safety element and the RHMP.

Stakeholder Engagement

Roseville has well exceeded the minimum DMA requirements for citizen involvement by formulating the RHMP through a variety of robust outreach measures. These included active participation of a 14-stakeholder Multi-Hazard Steering Committee that convened in August 2004 and met monthly through April 2005. The committee included representatives from businesses such as Hewlett-Packard, NEC, Union Pacific Railroad, Kaiser Permanente, and community-based organizations such as the Roseville Coalition of Neighborhood Associations. Three community workshops were held in the winter and spring of 2005, supplemented by local cable broadcasts, a webpage, press releases, mailings, and questionnaires, prior to the city council hearings that led to adoption.

Since then, the steering committee has met each July to monitor plan progress, review successes, address new state and federal requirements, offer advice on grant funding, and provide input into annual updates to the city council. Significant mitigation accomplishments noted by the committee at its July 2008 meeting included:

- Completion of the planting of 6,250 oak trees under the Native Oak Tree Planting Project, with another 1,000 to be planted in the upcoming fiscal year

- Acquisition (and removal of structures) of three Severe Repetitive Loss properties on Champion Oaks Drive with $227,996 in HMGP funds and $589,420 in Flood Mitigation Assistance funds (Figure 7.6)

- Relocation of the city emergency-operations center out of the 100-year floodplain

- Accreditation of the Roseville Building Department by the International Accreditation Service (IAS) under the International Building Code—the first building department to be so designated

- Completion of advanced National Incident Management System (NIMS) training for key city staff

- Activation by the city utilities department of California's first Stage One Water Conservation Alert, in response to the U.S. Bureau of Reclamation's drought-induced 25 percent reduction of the city's water supply from Folsom Dam. This was followed in February 2009 by a mandatory Stage Two Alert, requiring water customers to reduce use by 20 percent.

City of Roseville

Figure 7.6. *Acquisition of severe repetitive loss properties*

Leveraging Sustainability

An important selling point driving stakeholder engagement in this sustained series of mitigation-planning action cycles has been the knitting together of three city initiatives of substantial interest to the community.

1. *Economic development.* The RHMP is seen as a foundation for long-term resilience, where asset protection through hazard mitigation ensures continuity and quick resumption of the community's economy after a disaster. The city's economic development team also markets the City of Roseville as one of the safest in the region when preparing prospect packages and meeting with potential new businesses.

2. *Sustainability.* Through protection of community assets from loss, hazard mitigation ensures that economic, social, historical, environmental, and physical resources will be sustained.

3. *Green Communities Initiative.* By using hazard mitigation to preserve permanent open space, plant new forests, and reduce excess water consumption, Roseville seeks to be a responsible part of the global effort to minimize conditions contributing to greenhouse gas emissions and to adapt to climate change.

The continuing evolution of state policy related to climate change raises the question of how the evolving policies of Roseville and the state have influenced each other. The links are threefold. First, the legislature adopted AB 32 in 2006, drawing attention to the need for greenhouse gas reduction and carbon sequestration. Second, the 2007 California Multi-Hazard Mitigation Plan included several sections on climate change, including a series of illustrative statements on the types of hazards that would be exacerbated by climate change—flooding, wildfires, excess heat, and so on. Finally, Roseville leadership sees a direct connection between climate change adaptation and natural-hazard mitigation. Deputy City Manager Julia Burrows, who was active on the State Hazard Mitigation Team that helped prepare the 2007 state plan, has taken an interest in making the city more resilient as well as green. She got the annual plan-review committee focused on this issue in July 2008, seven months after the plan's adoption. Roseville was well ahead of the California Natural Resources Agency, which in late 2009 published the Climate Change Adaptation Strategy, reinforcing the 2007 SHMP.

The Story Continues

No story ever ends. Roseville is revising the RHMP, not only because of federal requirements but because of an inherent community need to look ahead based on experience and new information. City staff recently made scoping recommendations for the five-year RHMP update, under way with a $200,000 Pre-Disaster Mitigation grant and a $50,000 city match. In 2009, it began monthly meetings on the update, to be completed by 2010. The update will evaluate mitigation progress and issues emerging as important since 2005, such as climate change adaptability, potential failure of Folsom Dam and area dikes, and the inventory of buildings built before 1980.

The community has made major efforts in recent years to bring new economic life into the older downtown areas. The presence of older, seismically vulnerable unreinforced masonry (URM) buildings represents a potential business-continuity issue after an earthquake (Figure 7.7). The update will examine URM retrofit issues in response to state laws calling for local action. The initial RHMP addressed the issue of older, seismically vulnerable structures in some depth, placing the emphasis on age of the building inventory and less on type of construction, since URMs represent less than 1 percent of the city's inventory. The general plan primarily emphasized geologic investigations dealing with new construction. The RHMP update represents a step forward in focusing on the URM problem, prompted in part by the state law (SB 547), which calls for inventories and remediation of URM buildings as well as the realization of the economic benefits of business continuity in downtowns.

Significance for Others

Roseville represents the best convergence of local capacity to build and sustain disaster resilience through the support of state and federal laws and requirements, while always keeping the unique needs of the community uppermost. Its story demonstrates the use of best practices in planning and implementation. Building on a strong culture of preparedness and action, the community has its comprehensive general plan as a base for leveraging federal CRS benefits and FEMA Hazard Mitigation Assistance (HMA) financial incentives to accomplish mutually reinforcing objectives of hazard mitigation, economic development, and conservation. It reflects the strong commitment and collaboration of elected officials, local mitigation champions, and subject-matter experts in systematically setting sensible priorities for action and monitoring progress. Finally, it reflects skill within the city leadership in communicating the benefits of strong mitigation action to members of the community in a manner that generates ongoing willingness to act toward the common good.

Figure 7.7. Downtown area unreinforced masonry buildings

BERKELEY, CALIFORNIA
Kenneth C. Topping, FAICP

Berkeley, California, is an older city in the East Bay area of the San Francisco Bay region. Home to the University of California, an intellectual hub and symbol of liberalism, the community sits at the base of the wildfire-prone Berkeley Hills, astride the Hayward earthquake fault. From its inception, the community has suffered earthquake and wildfire disasters. Over the years, the community has sought to face its hazards, risks, and vulnerabilities and actively addressed hazard mitigation as a vital consideration for assuring sustainability of its unique social, economic, historical, cultural, and physical assets.

Mitigation of natural and human-caused hazards is written into both the comprehensive general plan and the Disaster Mitigation Plan. These documents both reflect the direction and progress of the ongoing mitigation program, under which the aging building inventory has been strengthened to reduce risks from the major earthquake expected on the Hayward and nearby San Andreas faults.

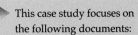

This case study focuses on the following documents:

- Disaster Mitigation Plan, City of Berkeley (June 2004)

- *General Plan: A Guide for Public Decision-Making*, City of Berkeley (December 2001)

- California Governor's Office of Planning and Research, General Plan Guidelines (2003)

- California Governor's Office of Emergency Services, 2007 State of California Multi-Hazard Mitigation Plan

In addition, the following people were interviewed:

- Arrietta Chakos, former Assistant City Manager

- Gil Dong, Fire Marshal, Berkeley Fire Department

- Dan Lambert, Senior Management Analyst, Planning and Development Department, City of Berkeley

- Debra R. Pryor, Fire Chief, City of Berkeley ◄

Figure 7.8. *The University of California–Berkeley campus, with the Golden Gate Bridge in the background*

Setting and Population

Berkeley is a city of about 100,000 people and part of a nine-county region that, with an estimated 7.4 million people, is now the sixth-most-populous metropolitan region in the United States. The Bay Area comprises a variety of subregions that are interconnected with six bridges, freeways, ferries, rail lines, and a rail rapid transit line and linked to the rest of the world by three airports and three container ports.

The East Bay Hills run from northwest to southeast approximately 60 miles, from the Carquinez Strait to Milpitas. At their base is the Hayward fault (Figure 7.9), which is capable of generating a magnitude 7.0 earthquake and bisects Berkeley, Oakland, and other nearby communities.

History

Founded as a town in 1878 following establishment of the University of California there in 1868, Berkeley became a city in 1909. The community experienced rapid growth after the 1906 San Francisco earthquake as thousands of evacuees resettled in the East Bay area. From then to World War II, it experienced its largest growth. Growth also continued during the war with an influx of shipyard workers employed in the nearby cities of Oakland and Richmond.

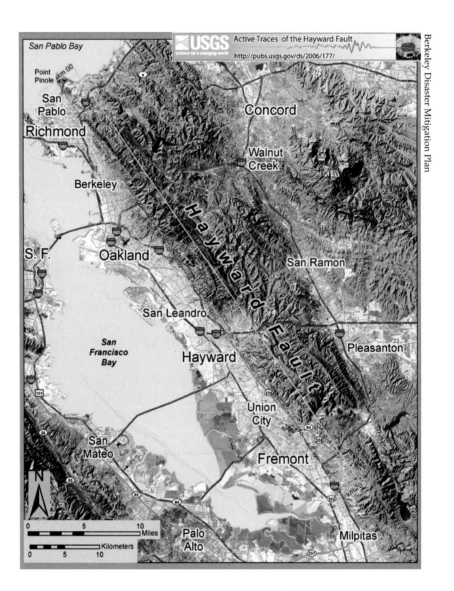

Figure 7.9. Regional fault systems

After World War II, the population declined. Between 1970 and 2000, the population dropped from 116,532 to 102,743, while the total number of dwelling units increased slightly from 46,160 to 46,875. Since vacant land had become limited, most new construction occurred as infill or redevelopment.

Disaster Experience

Most of Berkeley's natural disasters have been earthquakes or wildfires. Damage from the 1906 earthquake was substantially less in Berkeley than in San Francisco, where fires devastated many neighborhoods. Following the population growth in the years after that event, the Berkeley and Oakland portions of the East Bay Hills were extensively subdivided with small lots and narrow and winding dead-end roads. Because of the proliferation of a variety of flammable nonindigenous trees, such as eucalyptus and Monterey pine, and the prevalence of dry off-shore autumn winds, the hills have experienced devastating repetitive wildfires.

The most damaging wildfire in Berkeley started on September 17, 1923, in the hills to the northeast. It burned down into the community to Shattuck Avenue, destroying nearly 600 structures, including a library and a fire station (Berkeley 2004; see Figure 7.10). Since then, 14 large-scale fires have occurred in the Oakland Hills, of which seven originated in essentially one canyon area.

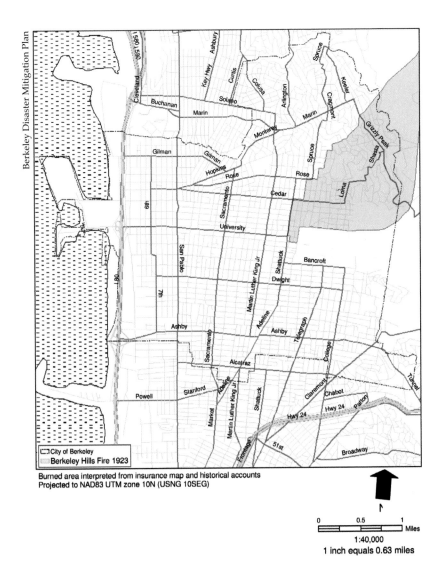

Burned area interpreted from insurance map and historical accounts
Projected to NAD83 UTM zone 10N (USNG 10SEG)

0   0.5   1   Miles
1:40,000
1 inch equals 0.63 miles

Figure 7.10. Berkeley Hills fire area, 1923

A more recent event that called the community's attention to its vulnerability to natural disasters was the magnitude 6.9 Loma Prieta earthquake, which rocked the Bay Area in October 1989, killing 63 persons, causing 3,757 injuries, and resulting in more than $10 billion in direct and indirect losses. Although Berkeley buildings experienced some damage, far greater losses were experienced in other communities, where elevated freeways collapsed, killing people and seriously disrupting the region's transportation network. The most visible damage was in San Francisco's Marina District, where the collapse of soft-story apartment buildings caught media attention. The downtown areas of Santa Cruz and Watsonville were also devastated.

Two years later, the Oakland Hills Fire (a.k.a. the Tunnel Fire) of October 1991 destroyed 3,400 homes in the Oakland portion of the East Bay Hills and 62 homes in the Berkeley portion. The firestorm was ignited due to a combination of factors, including an abundance of dry brush, flammable nonnative vegetation, nonfire-resistant building materials, drought, hot and dry weather, wind conditions, poor accessibility, and insufficient water pressure in some areas. Fire-fighting capability was seriously hampered by water-supply limitations in particular zones. This was compounded by the slow, difficult, and dangerous evacuation due to winding, narrow, and dead-end roads in the hills. Twenty-five people died. Lessons learned from the Oakland Hills Fire have since led to mitigation efforts in both Oakland and Berkeley, but a substantial wildland-urban interface (WUI) fire threat remains (Schwab et al. 1998).

Hazards and Vulnerability

Berkeley's greatest natural hazard is seismicity. Both the Hayward and San Andreas fault systems are susceptible to a high probability of a major earthquake in the next several decades. Development prior to the advent of modern building codes resulted in an inventory of structures highly vulnerable to earthquakes. These include unreinforced masonry (URM), concrete frame, tilt-up buildings built before the mid-1970s and buildings with "soft" stories (such as multiunit apartment buildings with ground-floor

Figure 7.11. *Hayward Fault in Berkeley Hills*

parking). The Association of Bay Area Governments (ABAG) estimated in 2002 that more than 13,300 housing units in Berkeley would be rendered uninhabitable by a major earthquake, resulting in a total shelter population of 8,530 (Berkeley 2004).

The community is bifurcated by the Hayward fault, which crosses directly beneath the university's Memorial Stadium (Figure 7.12). Given the enduring hillside WUI fire risk, Berkeley is vulnerable to a dangerous compound threat. Not only are many of Berkeley's older buildings at risk from severe shaking, but a magnitude 6.5 earthquake on the Hayward fault would also rupture gas and water lines, disrupt the power supply, and sever streets, increasing the likelihood of postearthquake fire spread within the community (Berkeley 2004). Fire following earthquakes caused extensive damage after the 1906 San Francisco earthquake and the 1995 Kobe earthquake (California OES 2007). Additionally, most Berkeley hillside development predates current codes and is vulnerable to landslide threat.

Learning from Disasters

Learning from these experiences during the last two decades, Berkeley has moved forward in accomplishing significant disaster-risk reduction, reaching out to actively encourage key stakeholders in the community to take responsibility for the safety of their homes, buildings, and community facilities. Table 7.2 chronicles the outcomes of significant public initiatives.

Building Retrofit Progress

Berkeley has distinguished itself as a community committed to integrating mitigation and preparedness into city life. Berkeley's significant achievements in strengthening older, seismically vulnerable public and private structures

Figure 7.12. Hayward Fault beneath Memorial Stadium

TABLE 7.2. SIGNIFICANT SAFETY IMPROVEMENT ACTIONS, 1989–2007

Year	Action	Outcomes
1989	Disaster Council formed	Established monitoring and advocacy for preparedness and mitigation
1989	URM inventory conducted	Risks identified and owners notified
1990	Board of Education reviews schools	Found life-safety hazards in 7 of 16 schools
1991	Fee-waiver program established for residential seismic retrofits	Waived permit fees on seismic retrofitting; ended in early 2000s due to budget constraints
1991	Transfer tax rebate ordinance for residential/URM retrofits adopted	Allowed rebate of one third of real estate transfer tax < $1,500 for seismic upgrade of dwellings
1991	Special assessment district created for Berkeley Hills	Assessed $50/parcel/year for fire-safety programs; ended due to state Proposition 218
1991	Strengthened requirements for hill-fire hazard zones	Stricter standards for roofing and other building materials
1991	Established mandatory URM retrofit program	Required retrofitting of URM buildings built before 1956 with five-plus units; 543 of 727 URM buildings in this category retrofitted
1992	Measure A approved	$158 million for school seismic retrofitting
1992	Measure G approved	$55 million for fire-station seismic retrofitting, creation of emergency operations center, and water-system improvements
1996	Soft-story and tilt-up building inventories developed	4,950 units soft-story housing (10% of housing) and 59 tilt-up structures identified
1996	Measure S approved	$45 million for seismic retrofit of Central Library and Martin Luther King, Jr. Civic Center Building (City Hall)
1997	University of California's SAFER Program established	$1.2 billion reconstruction plan for 27% of facilities needing seismic upgrading
1997	Uniform Building Code updated	Requirements increased for buildings close to active faults
2000	Tsukamoto Public Safety building completed	Hazard-resistant essential services building
2000	Measures AA and Q approved	$116.5 million for school safety program; tax measure for safety elements
2001	Martin Luther King Jr. Civic Center retrofit completed	City Hall housing key city government functions base-isolated for seismic safety
2002	Main Library retrofit complete	Major life-safety protection due to high usage
2005	Soft-story seismic upgrade ordinance adopted	Required owners of soft-story buildings of five-plus units to conduct studies, take other measures
2006	All fire stations seismically upgraded	Reconstruction of seventh fire station completed; six others seismically upgraded in prior years
2007	Neighborhood caches installed	8 major emergency-supply caches and 26 small caches placed in all council districts
2008	Student Housing Disaster Preparedness Program	Funded by [Bay Area Super Urban Area Security Initiative], mandated disaster preparedness training and caches placed in seven off-campus student dormitories.

Source: Berkeley Disaster Mitigation Plan

include the seismic retrofitting of its city hall and other critical facilities. The city has also encouraged property owners to retrofit most private URM buildings, as well as soft-story apartment buildings, through tax incentives. Between 1992 and 1998, approximately $3.5 million in property-transfer tax were waived for approximately 7,600 properties, while from 1992 to 1999 approximately $1.1 million in fees were waived for 4,100 seismic retrofitting permits. These incentives are credited with giving Berkeley one of the highest residential retrofit rates in the state (Figure 7.13).

As of March 2009, 543 (or 75 percent) of the 727 potentially hazardous URM buildings inventoried had been retrofitted under the Berkeley URM Retrofit Program. Remaining structures were at various stages. Only 11 structures had made no progress. Of these, eight had been issued citations. Although the retrofit program has emphasized the establishment of long-term relationships between the city and property owners, including efforts at education and provision of information, the city can, if necessary, enforce the ordinance provisions by placing properties into receivership.

Berkeley has also become a leader in Bay Area soft-story mitigation efforts promoted by ABAG, and it has made substantial progress on soft-story building retrofits. Of the 317 soft-story residential or mixed use buildings

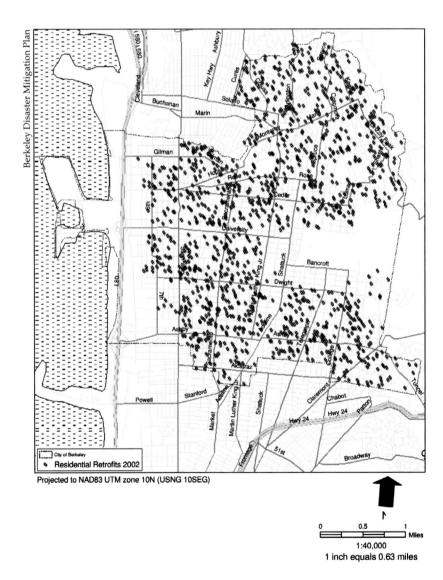

Figure 7.13. Seismically strengthened homes, 2002

with five or more units, 38 have been retrofitted, and 159 buildings are under notice to submit retrofit plans.

On account of such accomplishments, Berkeley has drawn regional and national attention. In 1998, it won the Western States Seismic Safety Council's award for Overall Excellence in Hazard Mitigation, as well as ABAG's Award for Retrofit Incentive Programs. In 1999, FEMA designated Berkeley as the Project Impact Model Community of the Year. And in 2002 and 2003, Berkeley was awarded special recognition from the Disaster Resistant California program and designated by the Governor's Office of Emergency Services as a model community.

Importance of State Law

Berkeley's mitigation progress has been driven by a combination of disaster experience, grassroots advocacy, good science, and progressive planning programs, as well as responses to state laws. California law does not promote a statewide growth-management system. Instead, it emphasizes local accountability for coordinated planning and implementation actions, which must meet broad state standards. State law includes requirements for a comprehensive general plan, with which local development decisions must be consistent.

The Berkeley general plan gathered fame in planning circles when the university and surrounding community figured prominently in T. J. Kent's book *The Urban General Plan* (1964), which significantly influenced development of California's general plan laws. At the heart of those laws is the requirement that all cities and counties must prepare and adopt a comprehensive general plan as a statement of future development goals, policies, and planned implementation actions. General plans must include seven elements: land use, circulation, housing, safety, conservation, open space, and noise. The safety element must reflect local hazards together with plans for their reduction. Not only must all general plan elements be consistent with one another, but implementation actions such as zoning, subdivisions, capital improvements, and permits must be consistent with the general plan, including the safety element.[1]

In addition to California general plan laws, other state hazard-mitigation laws passed in recent decades have guided local action commitments. Though more hazard-specific, such laws serve as a basic underpinning to the safety element of the general plan as well as implementation programs. Examples include:

1. The Earthquake Fault Zone Mapping Act of 1972, which requires the state geologist to prepare maps of major fault traces and zones and prohibits construction of new buildings used for human occupancy on the surface trace of active faults;[2]

2. Senate Bill 547, passed in 1986, which requires localities in the Uniform Building Code's Seismic Zone 4 to create an inventory of all URM structures and to develop a mitigation program;[3]

3. The Seismic Hazards Mapping Act, passed in 1990, which directs the Department of Conservation to map areas prone to liquefaction, earthquake-induced landslides, and amplified ground shaking and requires geotechnical investigations to formulate mitigation measures before issuance of building permits in mapped zones;[4] and

4. Assembly Bill 304, passed in 2005, which encourages localities to undertake surveys of soft-story buildings (defined as wood-frame multiunit residential structures constructed before January 1, 1978, where the ground-floor portion contains parking or other similar open floor space)

as potentially hazardous in an earthquake and authorizing adoption of ordinances governing seismic retrofits using nationally recognized codes.[5]

Within this statutory framework, the Berkeley general plan has served as the comprehensive policy foundation by which the community has advanced its overall disaster resilience and determined its hazard mitigation policy. Following extensive study, workshops, and public hearings starting in 1999 and ending with city council adoption in December 2001, the Berkeley general plan underwent comprehensive revision. The plan identifies seven major goals, the sixth of which states: "Make Berkeley a disaster-resistant community that can survive, recover from, and thrive after a disaster."

Goal 6 is elaborated within the Disaster Preparedness and Safety Element by six objectives, 28 policies, and 73 specific actions. Objectives include establishment of an effective emergency-response program, reduction of risks to people and property, and application of land-use planning and regulation to minimize exposure to hazards, with these three together focusing directly upon earthquake, wildfire, and flood loss reduction. Hazard mitigation policies and actions are found not only in the Disaster Preparedness and Safety Element but also in other elements, such as that for circulation.

First Local Mitigation Plan in California

Preceding the comprehensive revision of the Berkeley general plan was the Disaster Mitigation Act of 2000 (DMA 2000), by which localities across the country are required to prepare local hazard mitigation plans (LHMPs) as a precondition for receiving federal hazard mitigation grant funds. The Berkeley Disaster Mitigation Plan was prepared by staff and consultants with active involvement of community stakeholders starting in 2003 and concluding with city council adoption in June 2004.

The Disaster Mitigation Plan lists four objectives that are similar to the goals and objectives of the Disaster Preparedness and Safety Element of the Berkeley general plan. These objectives are:

A. Reduce the potential for life loss, injury, and economic damage to Berkeley residents from earthquakes, wildfires, landslides, and floods.

B. Increase the ability of the city government to serve the community during and after hazard events by mitigating risk to key city functions such as response, recovery, and rebuilding.

C. Protect Berkeley's unique character and values from being compromised by hazard events.

D. Encourage mitigation activities to increase the disaster resilience of institutions, private companies, and lifeline systems that are essential to Berkeley's functioning.

Tied directly to these objectives are 16 specific action items, including eight classified as high priority, six as medium priority, and two as low priority. Each action statement is accompanied by details such as identification of proposed activities, special environmental concerns, lead organization, timeline, and resources required.

The Disaster Mitigation Plan is notable in several ways. First, it was initiated in 2003 and adopted in 2004, well *after* the 2001 adoption of the Disaster Preparedness and Safety Element. Second, it became the first LHMP in California to be approved by FEMA. Third, the plan added a new focus on risk assessment and prioritized mitigation action not evident in the Berkeley general plan. This reflected DMA's emphasis on the need for localities to take greater responsibility for local hazards, risk, vulnerability assessment, and related mitigation action. This perspective is captured in the first paragraph of the plan's executive summary:

> Berkeley is a vibrant and unique community. But every aspect of the city—its economic prosperity, social and cultural diversity, and historical character—could be dramatically altered by a serious earthquake or fire. While we cannot predict or protect ourselves against every possible hazard that may strike the community, we can anticipate many impacts and take steps to reduce the harm they will cause. We can make sure that tomorrow's Berkeley continues to reflect our current values. This Mitigation Plan starts an ongoing process to evaluate the risks different types of hazards pose to Berkeley, and to engage the City and the community in dialogue to identify *which steps are most important to pursue to reduce these risks*. (Berkeley 2004)

Prioritizing Hazards and Actions

Thus, the Disaster Mitigation Plan differs from the general plan in two important aspects. First, it clearly identifies wildfires and earthquakes as the most critical hazards and risks faced by the city. Loss estimates in Section 3 of the plan convincingly demonstrate that earthquakes and wildfires have the greatest potential to cause large human and economic losses. Second, the plan emphasizes prioritized actions related to these hazards and risks. Although the Disaster Preparedness and Safety Element contained a suitably wide range of long-term policy and action statements, it provided little, if any, focus on which mitigation actions should be pursued in what sequence. Such prescriptions are clearly set forth in the Disaster Mitigation Plan and linked directly to each of its four objectives.

Prioritization of actions was developed through a process involving staff, council members, commissioners, residents, and other stakeholders in a Disaster Mitigation Summit, commission meetings, and a city council hearing. Actions prioritized as high or medium priority included: (1) having strong community support; (2) addressing the most critical hazards; (3) focusing on preserving life and reducing injury, which were given highest priority; and (4) strengthening the city's ability to provide essential emergency services to the entire community after a disaster, which was also weighted highly. Also included in top categories were recovery actions ensuring that the city's economic, educational, and governmental systems could resume normal functioning within 30 days of a major disaster.

Linkage to the General Plan

The Disaster Mitigation Plan and the general plan have an extraordinarily close linkage. Though organized differently, the two plans are characterized in many instances by almost interchangeable language. For example, under Objective A in the Disaster Mitigation Plan is High Priority Action A-1: "Strengthen or replace important city-owned and used buildings that are known to have structural weaknesses," which is followed by specific action language. This action statement is similar to Disaster Preparedness and Safety Element Policy S-20, Mitigation of Potentially Hazardous Buildings: "Pursue all feasible methods, programs, and financing to mitigate potentially hazardous buildings."

Similarly, under Disaster Mitigation Plan Objective A is Medium Priority Action A-7: "Reduce the vulnerability of residential areas located in the Hill Hazardous Fire Area [see Figure 7.14] to fires through implementation of the Subdivision Ordinance's merger provisions and through changes to the existing residential zoning laws and building code requirements." Such language is wholly consistent with the Disaster Preparedness and Safety

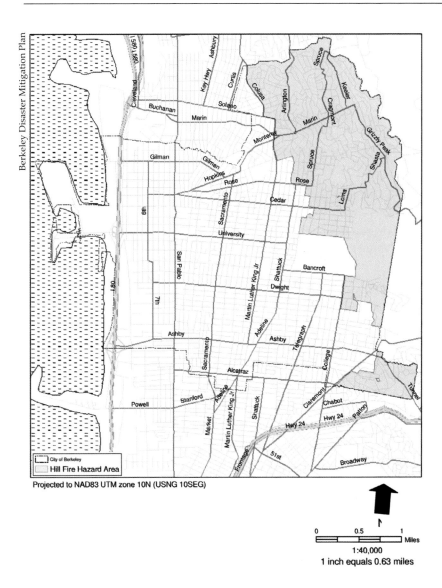

Figure 7.14. Hill fire hazardous area

Element's more generalized language in Objective 3: "Plan for and regulate the uses of land to minimize exposure to hazards from either natural or human-related causes and to contribute to a 'disaster-resistant' community," as well as more specific general plan policies and actions, including the element's Policy S-16, Residential Density in the Hills: "Consider changes to the existing residential zoning in high-risk, residential areas, such as the Hill Hazardous Fire Area, to reduce the vulnerability of these areas to future disasters," which is followed by more specific language.

Underscoring this direct relationship between the two plans is Disaster Mitigation Plan Medium Priority Action B-2: "Review and revise the Disaster Preparedness and Safety Element of the City's General Plan regularly. The Mitigation Plan will be included as an appendix of the General Plan, and will be reviewed frequently." This underscores a close relationship between the two plans in a coordinated process. California law offers postdisaster financial incentives to local jurisdictions that adopt their LHMPs as part of the general plan, but at present the two documents have not been jointly adopted.

Collaboration with Other Jurisdictions

Within and around Berkeley are a variety of independent jurisdictions to which state law separately assigns hazard mitigation responsibility. Examples include the Berkeley Unified School District, the University of California, Lawrence Livermore Laboratories, the East Bay Municipal Utilities District, and the East Bay Regional Park District. Most have been active partners with the city in jointly pursuing hazard mitigation projects.

For example, UC-Berkeley, which has more than 35,000 students and employs a workforce of more than 31,000, has a strong retrofit initiative, known as the Seismic Action Plan for Facilities Enhancement and Renewal (SAFER), that has resulted in significant improvements (Figure 7.15) since 1997.[6] SAFER involves an investment of $1 billion over 30 years to strengthen seismically vulnerable buildings, which accounted for more than a quarter of UC-Berkeley's inventory when the program started. The city and university have generally enjoyed a collaborative relationship, with the notable exception of a lawsuit filed by the city over expansion of an alumni facility at Memorial Stadium, which sits astride the Hayward fault (Figure 7.12, p. 101). In that case, the university prevailed, as the facility was found to be compliant with the Earthquake Fault Zoning Act because it was separated into two sections, one on either side of the fault.

Civic Culture and Hazards

Berkeley has an extraordinarily strong tradition of public engagement in the formulation, review, adoption, and execution of city policy. Berkeley long ago embraced a "culture of preparedness," which helped undergird the significant record of safety improvements summarized in Table 7.2. Making these achievements possible was a combination of intelligent forethought and awareness of risk on the part of residents, business owners, and other community stakeholders, buoyed by "champions" such as longtime mayor Tom Bates and Assistant City Manager Arrietta Chakos, together with a team of other committed building, planning, fire, and other staff professionals.

Adoption of the general plan in 2001 and the Disaster Mitigation Plan in 2004 were preceded in each case by extensive staff and citizen committee meetings, community stakeholder workshops, and formal public hearings before various commissions and the city council. For example, the Fire Safety and Disaster Preparedness Committee was heavily involved in the preparation of the Disaster Preparedness and Safety Element.

This same commitment has been evident in detailed implementation monitoring. Although the general plan has not been revised since 2001, the

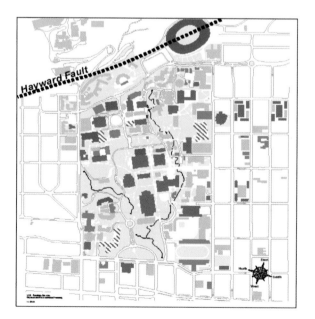

Completed buildings

Buildings in process

Still in planning stage

University of California–Berkeley

Figure 7.15. *Accomplishments of the UC–Berkeley SAFER program*

Disaster Mitigation Plan received minor updates in 2007 with information showing the city had made steady progress toward many of its objectives. The update added a progress statement for each action as well as suggestions on how to implement actions yet to be addressed.

The Story Continues

In the long run, Berkeley represents best practices in adaptive learning—a basic, often overlooked aspect of community planning. However, despite the culture of preparedness, the retrofit program fell on hard times with the 2009 national recession. The city, like many other communities, is now under severe budget pressure. The soft-story retrofit program has been defunded, as has a special safety-program coordinator position, upon which it depended for forward movement. Perhaps not coincidentally, a long-standing tension between that program and community rent-control advocates appears to have been exacerbated because of the cost impacts of seismic retrofits. With fewer "champions" available to promote mitigation, the Disaster Mitigation Plan update process (on a mandatory five-year cycle) has been more difficult.[7] Meanwhile, the Disaster Mitigation Plan details substantial mitigation work left to do. (See Figure 7.16.)

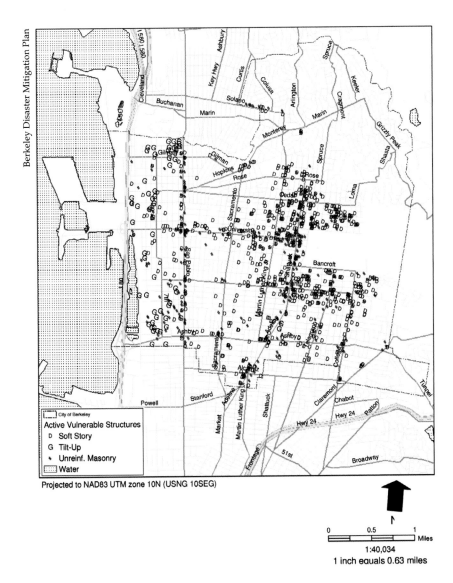

Figure 7.16. Remaining Vulnerable Structures, 2002

On the positive side, the city council on July 22, 2008, adopted an urgency ordinance that imposed a moratorium on most development in the Panoramic Hill area directly above the university within the Hill Fire Hazardous Area. The intent of the moratorium is to provide time to identify, formulate, and begin to implement a series of actions to address serious public-safety threats in that neighborhood. The scope of the initiative includes potential near-term actions as well as development of a strategy for long-range planning to address the area's underlying infrastructure and safety deficiencies. The process includes draft modifications to the zoning ordinance currently under review by the community, pending expiration of the moratorium.

Significance for Others

Berkeley is something unusual, at least in California if not elsewhere: an older city with a lively, ongoing, intense, and widely shared public discussion regarding its current state and future. It has accomplished a remarkable amount of preventive mitigation work and strengthening against natural hazards, leading to greater resilience without altering the unique character of the community. Much of Berkeley's remarkable success and mitigation progress have been based on its staff champions, engaged stakeholders, and political will, plus a determination to uncover community hazards and risks, particularly through detailed surveys of URM, soft-story, and other vulnerable construction.

The significant aspect of the Berkeley general plan is that this forward-looking statement of policies and actions was adopted as an outcome of the community's determination to take sustainability into its own hands by directly addressing hazards and resilience issues related to land-use planning. Berkeley has a desirably close link between its general plan and its Disaster Mitigation Plan, which together provide a factual and policy basis for mitigation and a logical sequence of prioritized action. In this respect, Berkeley is a national leader.

NOTES

1. California Government Code, sec. 65302 et seq.
2. Public Resources Code, sec. 2621
3. California Government Code, sec. 8875
4. Public Resources Code, sec. 2690 et seq.
5. Health and Safety Code, sec. 19160 et seq.
6. See http://berkeley.edu/about/fact.shtml and http://hrweb.berkeley.edu/workforce/census/WorkForceCensus_2008-10-31.pdf.
7. Former assistant city manager Arrietta Chakos is now with Harvard University's Kennedy School of Government.

CHAPTER 8

Case Studies: Small Towns and Rural Communities

BOURNE, MASSACHUSETTS
Ann F. Dillemuth

The Town of Bourne is a waterfront community of just under 20,000 people, located on Buzzards Bay at the gateway to Cape Cod. Bourne shares a predicament with countless other waterfront communities across the country: the bulk of its downtown district, the Village of Buzzards Bay, lies in a coastal flood-hazard zone. At the eastern end of Main Street, the 100-year flood elevation ranges from one to two feet above current street level; at the western end, it is at an average of five feet above.

Bourne's location puts it at high risk for hurricanes and coastal storms, both of which threaten the low-lying town with flooding from high winds, heavy precipitation, and storm surges. High-water marks recorded in Buzzards Bay from hurricanes in 1938 and 1954 reached 14.1 and 13.4 feet, respectively. More recently, 1991's Hurricane Bob caused a storm surge of nine feet in Buzzards Bay, with some measurements putting the high-water mark at 15 feet (Town of Bourne 2004).

Since the 1960s, revitalizing this downtown district has been a goal of town officials and community groups, but the flood hazard zone has persistently discouraged reinvestment and developer interest due to concerns about risk and uncertainty about floodproofing requirements and costs. Redevelopment in the zone is to some extent a necessity; physical and financial constraints prevent the wholesale relocation of the downtown. Thus, Bourne's focus has shifted toward how to regulate and incentivize such reinvestment in an environmentally sound and economically viable way. In recent years, Bourne has taken the first steps toward both mitigating flood hazards and catalyzing the downtown's renaissance.

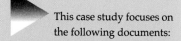

This case study focuses on the following documents:

- Town of Bourne Pre-Disaster Hazard Mitigation Plan (October 2004)

- Town of Bourne Local Comprehensive Plan (2008 update)

- Town of Bourne Zoning Bylaw (2008)

  - Section II, Use and Intensity Regulations. Part 2800. Downtown District.

  - Section III, General Regulations. Part 3110. Lowland Regulations - Flood Area Provisions.

- *Study of Flood Hazard Mitigation and Design for the Main Street Business District, Village of Buzzards Bay, MA.* Prepared by Kennen Landscape Architecture with OceanUS Design and Coastal Engineering (2007)

- *A Vision Plan for Bourne's Downtown: The Village of Buzzards Bay.* Prepared for the Bourne Financial Development Corporation by Stantec Planning and Landscape Architecture (2008)

In addition, interviews were conducted with the following people, who reviewed the case study to ensure accuracy:

- Ted Brovitz, Associate Planner, Stantec Planning and Landscape Architecture

- Stacey Justus, former Coastal Resources Specialist, Cape Cod Commission

- Kate Kennen, Landscape Architect, Kennen Landscape Architecture

- Coreen Moore, Town Planner, Town of Bourne, Massachusetts

- Sallie Riggs, Executive Director, Bourne Financial Development Corporation

- Sarah White, Hazard Mitigation Planner, Massachusetts Emergency Management Agency

- Kathy Zagzebski, President and Executive Director, National Marine Life Center ◄

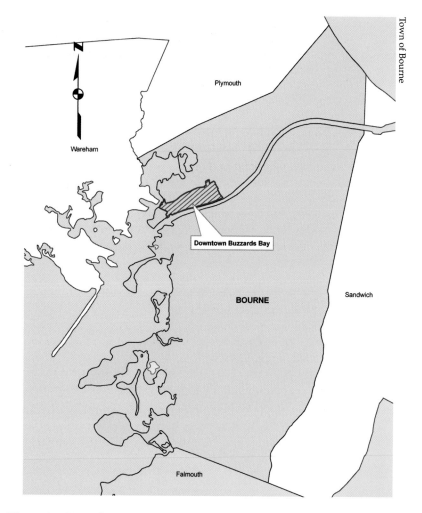

Figure 8.1. *Map of Bourne, Massachusetts*

Regional Support for Hazard Mitigation Planning

Massachusetts state statutes require municipalities with populations over 10,000 to create planning boards, though creating a master plan is not mandatory. There are no hazard planning requirements at the state level, but the Massachusetts Emergency Management Agency strongly encourages communities to create hazard mitigation plans, using the associated FEMA funding possibilities as an incentive. Because there is no county level of government in Massachusetts, smaller communities often rely on regional planning bodies or consultants for assistance with more progressive and proactive planning projects (White 2009). This was the case in Bourne.

Though officials and residents alike were well aware of Bourne's natural-hazards issues, mitigation had not been addressed in town policy or land-use regulations beyond the standard floodplain ordinance required by NFIP. This changed in the early 2000s. In 2002, Massachusetts's state hazard mitigation officer (SHMO) asked Stacey Justus, the coastal resource specialist at the Cape Cod Commission (CCC), the area's regional planning and land-use regulatory agency, to facilitate the region's participation in Project Impact, a FEMA program on building disaster-resilient communities. Working with emergency managers within the 15-town region, they produced the 2004 *Cape Cod Emergency Preparedness Handbook*.

At the SHMO's urging, Justus then applied for and received funding to create a Pre-Disaster Mitigation (PDM) plan for the region. The scope of work included helping the 15 towns in the CCC's jurisdiction develop their own local plans. Nine of Cape Cod's 15 towns opted to join the process—more often than not because a local official was personally motivated to get the work done. In Bourne, that person was Coreen Moore, the town planner (Justus 2009).

Justus met monthly with the coordinating officials of the nine towns, walked them through the PDM planning process step by step, and gave them "homework assignments" each month. The CCC used its GIS capabilities to develop risk and vulnerability assessment (RVA) maps for the project, but each town was responsible for developing its own local process and team, inventorying its needs, and creating its own action plans. The process took a year and a half. Bourne's Local Hazard Mitigation Plan (LHMP) was adopted by the town's board of selectmen on October 26, 2004.

Creating the Local Hazard Mitigation Plan

To create the plan, the board created a Disaster Hazard Mitigation Committee, which consisted of the town's existing Local Emergency Management Planning Committee as well as the town planner, town engineer, and the building inspector. Community groups, local businesses, and local media were also represented on the 27-member committee.

The LHMP (Town of Bourne 2004) identifies flooding (including flooding and high tides from northeasters and storm surges from hurricanes), wind-related hazards (including hurricanes and coastal storms), and coastal

TABLE 8.1. HAZARD IDENTIFICATION MATRIX

Natural Hazard	Likelihood of Occurrence 0 = Unlikely 1 = Possible 2 = Likely 3 = Highly likely	Location 1 = Small area 2 = Medium area 3 = Large area	Impacts 1 = Limited 2 = Significant 3 = Critical 4 = Catastrophic	Hazard Index
Flood	3	3	3	9
Wind Related				
Hurricane	3	3	3	9
Coastal Storms	3	2	3	8
Winter Storms	2	3	3	8
Fire Related				
Drought	1	3	2	6
Wildfires	2	3	2	7
Urban Fires	1	1	1	3
Shoreline Erosion	3	3	3	9
Geologic Hazards				
Associated Landslides of Coastal Banks	2	2	2	6
Earthquakes	0	3	1	4
Tornadoes	0	1	1	2

Source: Town of Bourne

erosion as the most significant natural hazards facing Bourne. Wildfire was also seen a potential threat due to the proximity of abundant, unfragmented forest habitat. The plan lists 19 action items, the majority of which address flooding problems. These include enhancing floodplain management activities; joining the NFIP's Community Rating System (CRS) program; acquiring and preserving extremely flood-prone properties in the town; revising the town's floodplain zoning bylaw; and providing public outreach and education on hazard mitigation.

Hazards in Local Planning and Land Development Documents

Although Bourne's revised Local Comprehensive Plan (Town of Bourne 2006) does not incorporate the LHMP directly, its Coastal Resources Element addresses flood hazards. The plan notes that much of the Village of Buzzards Bay lies within the 100-year floodplain and the projected Sea, Lake, and Overland Surges from Hurricanes (SLOSH) zone for hurricanes in Categories 1 through 4, but it recognizes that revitalization of this area may nevertheless be an important part of the town's future economic prosperity. It calls upon the town to "identify and promote sound construction and design strategies that would allow redevelopment within the floodplain without undue risk to public safety or property."

The first of three Coastal Resources Policies reads:

- Ensure that future development and modification of existing development is properly sited and designed to minimize flood hazards and maintain the ability of coastal landforms to migrate properly.

The third of three Highest Priority Actions for Coastal Resources is:

- Develop a Coastal Hazard Management Plan and identify necessary actions to address the effects of weather damage, projected sea-level rise, bank erosion, and sand migration.

A Second Priority Action for Coastal Resources is:

- Revise the Floodplain Zoning Bylaw to reflect the action items of the Bourne Pre-Disaster Hazard Mitigation Plan adopted in October 2004.

Bourne's zoning bylaw was updated in early 2009 to amend sections addressing flood hazard issues (Town of Bourne 2009). The Flood Area Provisions (Section III, Part 3110) apply the State Building Code's new standards for Flood Resistant Construction (780 CMR 120.G) to new construction or substantial improvement within the A and V zones on the town's Flood Insurance Rate Maps. These standards, revised in 2008, conform to the NFIP and adopt post–Hurricane Katrina FEMA recommendations for construction in flood hazard zones. The bylaw also prohibits mobile homes and campers in A and V zones, as well as alteration of sand dunes in V zones.

One important amendment to the Flood Area Provisions was the addition of a cumulative cost provision regarding substantial improvement to structures. Under the old bylaw, property owners who wanted to substantially upgrade their structures could avoid compliance with mandatory floodproofing requirements by requesting a series of building permits, each under the 50 percent value threshold that would trigger those requirements. The cumulative-cost clause helps to close that loophole by considering all permits for a structure within a two-year period to be a single improvement.

Implementation

The completion of Bourne's LHMP set the town on the road to implementation, but action steps are still tackled only when and if funding becomes available (Moore 2009). Indeed, Justus has seen implementation to be a

FLOOD ZONE TYPE

Parcels with Flood Zone
Information Not Included

VE17
AE16
AE15
AE14
XF
XO

Extent of Flood Data from FIRM Maps Digitized for this Study

Bourne Bridge

Belmont Circle

Town Hall

Perry Ave

Cape Cod Canal

Main Street

Bypass Road

Park

Railroad Bridge

Memorial Circle

Kennen Landscape Architecture

Figure 8.2. Summary of FEMA Flood Insurance Rate Map Flood Zones in Buzzards Bay, the downtown core of the Town of Bourne. The A and V zones make up the 100-year floodplain.

stumbling block for most of the towns in the region. She notes that FEMA is ready to fund shovel-ready projects, while LHMPs address broad planning concepts. Assistance is not currently available to help towns with the planning and technical design work necessary to bridge the gap between plan and project (Justus 2009).

Despite these obstacles, Bourne has taken substantial steps toward mitigation of the natural hazards it faces. To address the threat of wildfire, mitigation and maintenance plans were created for two high fire-risk areas in the town. Bourne is also in the early stages of applying to join the CRS program.

The town is looking at design strategies for existing open space to address flood hazard issues. A design competition was held for the park that occupies part of the east end of the downtown area, where 100-year flood levels range from six to 10 feet above street level. The entries integrated elements of flood mitigation into their designs, focusing on water elements and wetland preservation and envisioning the area as a holding area for floodwaters. Progress on a final plan for the park is slow, however, hindered by the need to coordinate agendas of multiple entities and by the perennial problem of funding.

Perhaps the most innovative and valuable step the town has taken has been commissioning a flood-hazard mitigation report for the Village of Buzzards Bay, which has not been able to attract much-needed reinvestment because of the uncertainties developers face in the flood hazard zone, the largest on Cape Cod. How much or what kind of development is the town willing to approve? What sorts of floodproofing requirements are required, and how much extra cost does that create?

The economic development community in Bourne has taken up the mitigation issue. Before the Bourne Financial Development Corporation, an agency created for the town by the state legislature in 2000, could successfully recruit outside investment, it had to create an environment conducive to redevelopment—which meant addressing a host of issues (Riggs 2009). The BFDC set up the Main Street Steering Committee (MSSC) to focus on revitalization of the downtown district.

The MSSC and the town were able to leverage state funding to bring in outside consultants with an objective view and professional expertise. The MSSC coordinated the creation of a Vision Plan for the downtown and a wastewater management study to address the aging sewer system in the district. In addition, the Buzzards Bay Village Association commissioned a transportation study. The town obtained a Smart Growth Technical Assistance grant to fund a study of mitigation options for the downtown flood-hazard zone. The final report (Kennen Landscape Associates et al. 2007) has proven to be a valuable document that distinguishes Bourne's mitigation planning efforts.

Study of Flood Hazard Mitigation and Design for the Main Street Business District
The report maps the downtown flood-hazard conditions and summarizes relevant town, state, and federal regulations, including FEMA mitigation requirements for structures located in A and V zones. It then lays out a flood-hazard analysis flowchart. By answering simple questions regarding flood zone location, sill elevation, existence of a basement or crawl space, building type, and construction date, parcel owners can start to determine how likely it is that their property is compliant with flood regulations. If it is not, the flowchart directs users to an illustrated list of mitigation design solutions specifically tailored to that property (Kennen 2009).

A following section lays out regulatory requirements and a smorgasbord of design solutions. These range from parcel-level solutions, such as filling basements and elevating first floors of structures, to comprehensive village and block-scale proposals, such as moving the downtown center to higher ground.

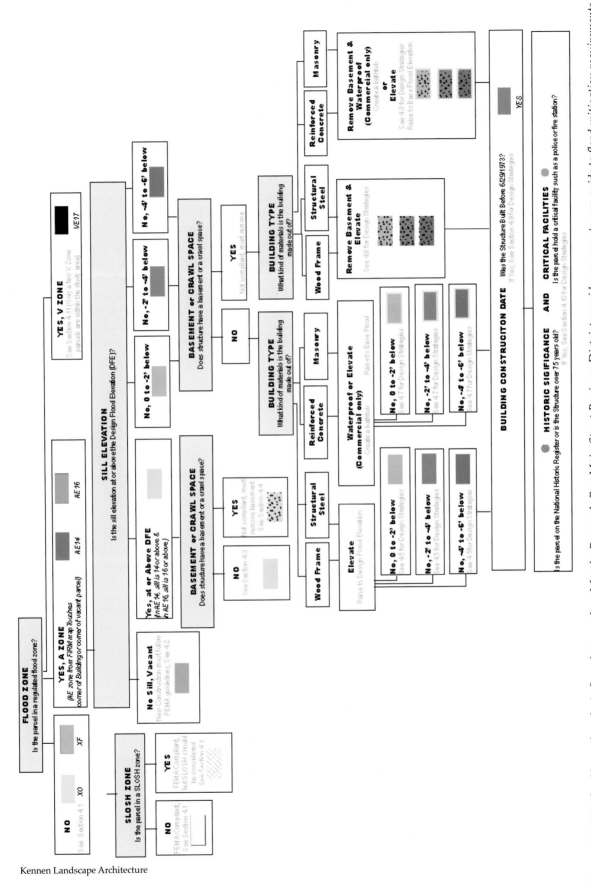

Figure 8.3. *This flood hazard analysis flow chart produced for the Buzzards Bay Main Street Business District provides an easy-to-use guide to flood mitigation requirements for construction in regulated FEMA flood zones.*

Kennen Landscape Architecture

(See Figure 8.4.) The report is therefore relevant to individual property owners as well as entities with larger assembled landholdings. Finally, the study lays out a number of action items, including revising the master plan and zoning bylaws to implement recommended mitigation strategies.

The study is an extremely valuable resource for the town, the BFDC, current property owners, and potential investors. The study's value has been proven by the experience of the National Marine Life Center (NMLC), the first entity to launch a redevelopment project in the downtown district.

The NMLC, founded in 1995 as a nonprofit marine animal hospital with an educational and science component, had selected Bourne's downtown district for a hospital and educational center because of the available space close to the waterfront—a rare resource on the Cape. The town, eager to attract the project, sweetened the deal by offering a long-term lease on an old oil-transfer station property donated by ExxonMobil.

When existing buildings on the site succumbed to structural damage brought on by years of neglect, efforts to renovate those structures shifted to the opportunities provided by new construction. NMLC's architects used the Flood Hazard Mitigation Study to revise the master plan for the project and work creatively with the new floodplain zoning regulations to design elegant solutions. Rather than putting the buildings on stilts and surrounding them with floodwalls, the new plans (see Figure 8.5) play with finished floor elevations, providing multiple levels for uses with varying flood-level-height requirements (Zagzebski 2009). More information on this project can be found at www.nmlc.org.

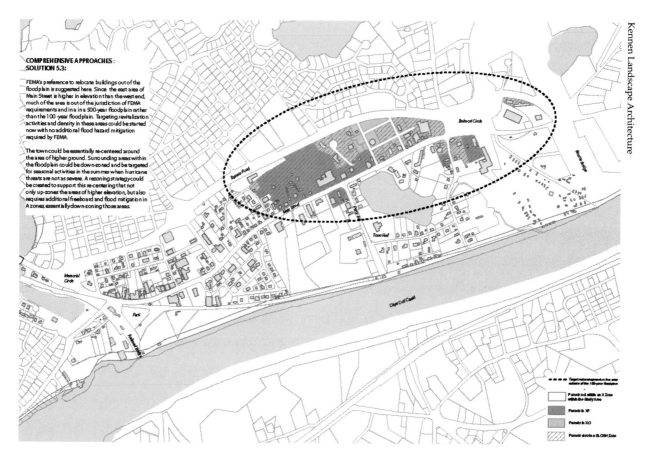

Figure 8.4. *One comprehensive design strategy proposed by the Flood Hazard Mitigation Study is to relocate the downtown center to higher ground outside the 100-year floodplain.*

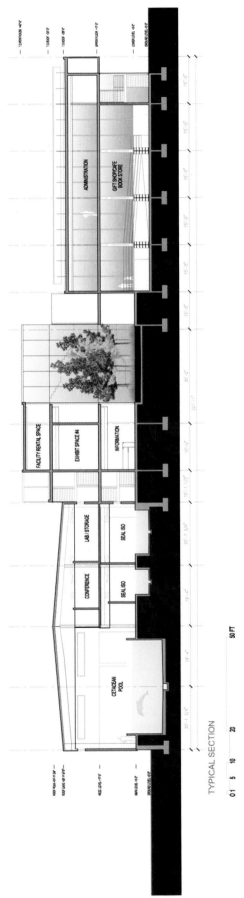

Cosestudi and National Marine Life Center

Figure 8.5. *The architectural design for the National Marine Life Center's new marine hospital and educational center creatively responds to flood hazard regulations in Bourne's downtown center.*

The MSSC and the town hope that this redevelopment project might be the catalyst for additional reinvestment in the downtown. Moore describes downtown property owners as being in a "wait-and-see mode" after decades of depressed values and little activity. As Sallie Riggs (2009), BFDC's executive director, sees it, the MSSC "needs to financially and psychologically get people over that hump." The Flood Hazard Mitigation Study goes far in educating potential investors about the status and requirements applicable to downtown parcels.

The study was also incorporated into a BFDC-commissioned vision plan for the downtown area (Stantec Planning and Landscape Architecture 2008), which used it to shape recommendations for downtown redevelopment. These included setting aside V zones as off-limits to new development, refocusing the central business district toward the eastern end of Main Street (where only one to two feet of extra elevation is required for floodproofing), and exploring ways to raise sections of Main Street and create multilevel mixed use buildings with parking below, retail and outdoor decks on the second and third floors, and residential above. (See Figure 8.6.)

The plan's Action Plan and Implementation Schedule calls for adopting a floodplain-permitting assistance program and encourages use of the Flood Hazard Mitigation Study by downtown property owners. According to Ted Brovitz (2009), the planner who headed the study, Bourne is unusual among the historic New England towns he has worked with in its willingness to look at its downtown as an "open book." Residents and officials have faced the reality of existing constraints in order to envision a new and different future for their downtown.

Bourne Financial Development Corporation/Stantec Planners and Landscape Architects

Figure 8.6. *The Vision Plan produced for Downtown Buzzards Bay envisions renovation of existing structures, such as the Christopolus Building shown here, to comply with floodplain regulations.*

A further product of the visioning process was a proposed downtown-district zoning bylaw implementing a form-based code to guide mixed use redevelopment according to smart-growth principles. The town approved the bylaw in October 2008, making Bourne the third town in Massachusetts to incorporate a form-based code. Now the MSSC is working on expediting the permitting process for downtown projects, as well as helping investors overcome the costs of rehabilitating their existing structures to meet the new flood mitigation requirements. Possibilities suggested in the Vision Plan include revolving loan funds or tax relief for flood improvements.

Lessons for Others

Bourne's experience can provide valuable lessons for other communities. Bourne is not unique in having significant areas located in known hazard zones. Developers and public officials alike recognize that building in these areas is not ideal, but there are few options, due to physical and economic constraints.

According to Moore, the most important thing a community can do to address hazard mitigation is to be aware of the current situation and what can be done to mitigate existing hazards. When current landowners have questions or potential investors voice concerns about flood hazard issues, the town's Flood Hazard Mitigation Study provides information and recommendations (Moore 2009).

From the developer's viewpoint, the Flood Hazard Mitigation Study demonstrates that there are creative, sound, cost-effective strategies for development that accord with strict flood-hazard mitigation requirements (Zagzebski 2009). Financial incentives for flood mitigation improvements may only improve the outlook (Riggs 2009).

From her regional perspective, Justus sees Bourne as unique in tying economic development to hazard mitigation through the efforts of the MSSC. "Hazard mitigation is an economic development issue—it doesn't make sense to invest in redevelopment if hazards will ultimately endanger your investment," she says. She credits the economic development community for generating more buy-in and interest in hazard mitigation than the town planner and emergency manager were able to achieve on their own (Justus 2009). With the state building code's flood-resistant construction upgrades, the town's recently strengthened floodplain regulations, and the downtown Flood Hazard Mitigation Study, Bourne is working to ensure that the mitigation of natural hazards will play a large role in the redevelopment and economic revitalization of its downtown.

MORGAN COUNTY, UTAH

Rebecca Little Leitschuh

Imagine you are the county planner or an elected official in a small, rural community that has just experienced a landslide within one of its new subdivisions. The land has already been platted and sold for development, but you have the responsibility to protect residents' welfare and lives. A building moratorium is not a realistic long-term solution politically, and it would likely result in a lawsuit over private land rights. In an attempt to protect residents, their property, and public improvements while not strictly prohibiting development of any lot, you create an ordinance requiring property owners in known hazard areas to submit a geologic hazard report prior to receiving a building permit. This report must be prepared by a licensed geologist and detail proper design and construction practices to safeguard against potential risks. This seems like a successful way for the municipality to gain control over potentially hazardous development practices, while

The State of Utah requires adherence to the following by local jurisdictions potentially affected by hazard mitigation:

- Pre-Disaster Mitigation Plan

- Emergency Operations Plan

- International Fire Code

- Wildland Urban Interface Code

- International Building Code

- County Comprehensive Emergency Management Plan

This case study focuses on the following documents for Morgan County:

- Morgan County General Plan

- Eight area plans, included in the general plan

- Sensitive Areas District documents

- Geologic Hazards Ordinance

- Subdivision Design and Regulations

In addition, the following individuals were interviewed:

- Brad Bartholomew, Mitigation Planner/Recovery Officer, State of Utah

- Sherrie Christensen, Community Development Director, Morgan County

- Grant Crowell, AICP, Director of Planning and Development Services, Morgan County

- DeeEll Fifield, Pre-Disaster Mitigation Planner, Wasatch Front Regional Council

- Dave Manning, GIS Specialist, Morgan County

- Linda Manning, Director, Morgan County Historical Society

- Jana Peay, Morgan County Librarian

guaranteeing property owners the right to develop their land in a safe manner, subject to a number of pertinent conditions.

Now imagine that you are the owner of one of these lots, a parcel in a new subdivision in the bucolic hills, surrounded by a panorama of streams, trees, and small-farm agriculture. However, after purchasing this land with the intention of building your home on it, you are informed that you will now be required to pay for an additional report and the cost of its review, complete with mitigation measures. Only after the county approves your report can you receive a building permit. You have submitted multiple revised reports, worked with multiple engineers and geologists, and $30,000 later the county still refuses to issue you a building permit because their geologist holds that the findings in the report are not supported by adequate data and that the report is incomplete.

This scenario confronted Morgan County, Utah, in 2005, when a subdivision in the Mountain Green area, zoned for residential development, became the scene of a slow-moving, deep-seated landslide that damaged the proximal properties. The landslide triggered more proactive planning and new mitigation policies, but the retroactive application of the policy has polarized the community and provided a valuable lesson for planners and elected officials. According to Grant Crowell, Director of Planning and Development Services for Morgan County, "The story has been the struggle with the moral issue of what should we do when we see things move, and what is fair, and at what cost?"

Background

Morgan County lies in Utah's Wasatch Mountains. A river valley surrounded by lush mountains, its 13 streams eventually enter the Great Salt Lake via the Weber River. However, the natural geologic and climatic events that engender this beauty also bring natural hazards, which are compounded by the presence of humans.

Morgan County is under considerable development pressure because of its natural beauty, open land, opportunities for recreation (Figure 8.7), and

Figure 8.7. *Fly-fishing in Morgan County*

proximity to highly developed Salt Lake City, 30 miles to the southwest. This is a recent trend, since the county has been fairly inaccessible and unpopulated throughout its history due to the steep mountain peaks and narrow river valleys. To this day, its roads are mostly two-lane, except for the main arterial of Interstate 84.

The county population was only 8,357 in 2007. Most adult residents work outside the county. There is only one major industry at present, Holcim Cement, on Lost Creek Road, which recently required reconstruction significant enough to use up the county's entire allocation of highway funds for three years. Given the choice between improving roads countywide and jeopardizing access to the largest tax-contributing industry, the county opted to rebuild Lost Creek Road in the summer of 2009.

Morgan County is susceptible to a variety of natural hazards and faces an increasing threat of more significant disasters if development increases in high-hazard areas. According to the Wasatch Front Natural Hazards Pre-Disaster Mitigation Plan, the county is at highest risk of a "catastrophic" earthquake (Wasatch Front Regional Council 2003). Four earthquakes have been detected since 1953, but because of their minimal intensity and the limited number of built structures in the county, little damage has occurred. Flooding is another hazard Morgan County faces, from cloudbursts, heavy snowfall runoff, and the possibility of one of its two major reservoir dams rupturing. This last possibility is projected to cause the greatest economic loss and loss of life. The county also faces a wildfire hazard, though it is of relatively minimal concern as the population in the wildland-urban interface is small. Finally, the county is highly vulnerable to landslides in specific areas.

The Mountain Green area was designated as prone to landslides in the 1970s, but in the late 1990s a developer worked with a former state geologist who reported that conditional use permits would sufficiently mitigate landslide risks (Christensen 2008). The developer thus gained approval to plat and develop the land. However, in 2005 the land began to slide, affecting three homes and additional vacant lots on Creekside Drive (Figure 8.8). Although only three structures were damaged, had more houses been completed the impact would have been felt across three subdivisions, totaling about 100 lots. Because the landslide was slow moving, it took the county a year and a half to collect enough evidence to condemn the compromised

Figure 8.8. *In this diagram of the Creekside landslide, the areas in red show where movement occurred.*

residences. The county's Planning and Development Services Department was confronted with the problem of keeping residents safe, even removing some from harm, while not provoking takings claims.

The planning department thus introduced a Geologic Hazards Ordinance, which met little initial resistance because it provided fair opportunities for owners to prove their lots were sound through engineering geologist reports and mitigation plans. However, according to Grant Crowell, the ordinance has turned politically difficult. He says, "We had to hire geologists, and we had to require property owners to pay for geologists," which turned into a "battle of the experts." In addition, the county council was concerned with the financial burden placed on property owners. Crowell says that a "balancing point between regulations and rights" must be found and that the paradigm would be different in rural areas than in urban ones. Because the developer deflected the conditional use requirements onto the individual home owners instead of addressing the natural hazards in the subdivision development plan, the home owners were stuck with the land and the costs of the necessary engineering measures to gain approval to build. Moreover, home owners faced the possibility of never qualifying for a building permit because of physical or financial limitations. Property owners were sold a lemon but could not necessarily afford enough sugar to make lemonade.

The county is trying to reconcile some of the problems that grew out of the geologic hazards ordinance through a second draft of the code, which includes pages of evaluation techniques and technical references, so as to set more specific parameters and standards for the report. Crowell says the county council remains conflicted, but he hopes it will take an informed position and continue to support the staff that must implement what it passes.

The case of Morgan County demonstrates how small local governments with minimal staff and a low tax base can integrate components of hazard mitigation into their planning. Beyond the geologic hazards ordinance, the county incorporates risk-reduction practices throughout its general plan, with mitigation objectives and strategies included in chapters on the environment, land use, community character, and public services. Morgan County further prioritizes hazard mitigation techniques by developing implementation tools, like codes and ordinances, to regulate development in designated high-risk areas. Finally, because Morgan County consistently prioritizes the community vision of protecting farmland and open space, it indirectly connects residents' values to mitigation, thereby gaining more public support.

Planning Staff

The Morgan County Planning and Development Services Department consists of four staff members, whose duties include code enforcement, GIS, planning-commission meeting administration, and the creation and implementation of plans. The department is responsible for ensuring that the zoning code, ordinances, and development review policies support the goals and objectives stated in the Morgan County General Plan. The planning staff holds meetings with those directly affected by changes to the county code or the implementation of new regulations. They have found that public support is more readily gained by fully explaining in an open setting how these changes protect residents' lives, property, and community values. For example, the Wildland-Urban Interface (WUI) building standards, which the county adopted in 2007, were met with little resistance from home builders and developers because residents recognized their increased safety and developers recognized the increased desirability of safer buildings. The State of Utah has promulgated the WUI code since 2005 with a carrot-and-stick approach by withholding funds for hazards-related activities in counties that fail to adopt the code.

Hazard Mitigation

The sections that follow introduce some of Morgan County's efforts to mitigate damages to life and property. Morgan County consistently employs two tactics: generating action items to reduce risk while demonstrating an allegiance to community character and vision.

Community Vision

Morgan County's general plan establishes a community vision that promotes policies in accord with the community character. The vision reflects the values of the first settlers who relocated from Salt Lake City to the more remote area in the 1880s and braved the risks for the accompanying benefits of open space, privacy, and fertile land for agriculture. The community vision focuses on preserving the county's rural and agricultural integrity in the face of recent development pressures, thus prioritizing rural character as the overarching policy goal. According to the general plan, "Growth will come and must be compatible with the rural, residential, agricultural, and small-town character of Morgan County" (Morgan County 2007).

However, while this vision is shared by longtime residents, mostly descendants of the original settlers, it conflicts with the vision of newer, exurban Salt Lake City residents who are attracted to the beauty of Morgan County and access to recreational activities like skiing and fishing. These new inhabitants favor policies promoting development of infrastructure, expansion of services such as schools and waste removal, and creation of subdivisions. Thus, the community values in the general plan do not fully represent the values of the entire community.

Nevertheless, the community vision does help reduce exposure to risk by discouraging development that compromises natural resources, open space, and natural beauty. This includes anything that would reduce the scenic beauty (e.g., building on fault lines, which form the ridges that protrude from the forest cover) or quality of life (e.g., impairing clean air, clean water, or public safety). Additionally, it protects environmental resources (e.g., water quality, environmental corridors, hillsides, open space, soils, wetlands, and floodplains), which sometimes help minimize hazards such as flooding, erosion, and landslides. Also, because the community vision encourages policies that allow farmers to stay on their land, it has the effect of suppressing residential subdivisions. The community vision statement also demands that new development and growth pay its own way for infrastructure expansion. While no enforcement mechanism is offered, this disincentive could serve to slow the conversion of land. Overall, the community vision slows the rate of subdivision and lessens the population exposed to risks within sensitive areas.

Comprehensive Planning

The approach to hazard mitigation in Morgan County's general plan is notable for two reasons. First, its goals commonly address natural hazards across subject lines, from community character to land use to public services and facilities. The environment chapter is even more robust, including holistic coverage of all risks and descriptions of different stakeholders. It succeeds in including mitigation measures in environmental concerns such as aesthetics, quality of life, or riparian corridors. Second, the goals and policies are implemented into action items. Here is a summary of broad mitigation themes that appear in the general plan.

Development. The general plan includes four different degrees of mitigation relating to development. Individually and combined, they keep subdivisions and expanding infrastructure out of sensitive areas and rural land, some of which is also risk-prone.

- *Agricultural operations given high-priority use of land.* Encourages farmers and ranchers to stay on their land. Preserves grazing land that was previously left undeveloped because of the hazardous nature of the land (e.g., landslides).

- *New development and growth must pay own way for infrastructure expansion.* Introduced in the Community Vision statement, but no elaboration on how this is to be implemented.

- *Memorandum of understanding.* Written agreement that rural property owners must sign setting expectations for levels of service. This memorandum says that the county will not provide urban levels of service to remote areas.

- *All future development on least-sensitive areas of the lands involved.* The method of selecting "sensitive areas" is not defined.

Hillsides. Hillsides are attractive locations on which to build homes because of their beauty and remoteness, but they may also be susceptible to wildfires, landslides, and earthquakes. Morgan County has established hillside standards that prevent future construction from compromising soil stability or placing homes on "scenic views" or high-risk overhangs. The standards also require professional studies to ascertain the risks and determine appropriate mitigation measures.

- *Discourage development on hills and ridge lines.* Prevents obtrusive development. While the rationale is aesthetic, it omits building on precipices, some of which are susceptible to earthquakes and landslides.

- *Prohibit development on natural slopes of 25 percent or greater and on unstable soils.* This includes areas of slope instability or with avalanche history.

- *Require geotechnical studies in areas of soil instability.*

- *Develop hillside grading ordinance.* Intended to minimize hazards of erosion and slope failure; there are no further details in the general plan.

Figure 8.9. View of Morgan Valley from a hillside

Courtesy of Morgan County Historical Society

Vegetation. Vegetation regulation relates to hillside standards but also applies to the broader community. It can be used as a mitigation measure before, during, and after development by requiring specific types of vegetation to prevent erosion or wildfire and by mandating the preservation of existing vegetation in a new development.

- *Must preserve or create adequate buffers along all waterways and wetlands.* While aimed at aesthetics and water quality, preservation of buffers contributes to soil stability, especially on steep terrain. The vegetation up-slope from the development is a more important consideration than that between development and a waterway.

- *Retain the maximum amounts of existing vegetation stands.* Areas with sensitive lands must be designated before construction and remain undisturbed. Straight-line removal is discouraged via a focus on preserving native vegetation. Existing vegetation stabilizes soil and minimizes erosion, which could be exacerbated by development.

- *Adopt logging standards on private land to minimize adverse impacts.* Standards may minimize soil erosion and sedimentation on land not managed by the county, which in turn may reduce stormwater runoff and landslides.

- *Require fire-resistant landscape buffers or zone buffers in high-risk hazard areas.* These include the careful spacing of shrubs and trees, clearing of fuels such as dead trees and leaves, and selecting fire-resistant vegetation as identified in Firewise Communities publications.

Waterways. Morgan County does not make many references to flood mitigation or even its vulnerability to flooding. Although the county is susceptible to riverine flooding and the potential collapse of any major reservoir, in the absence of such disasters the county has adopted secondary flood-mitigation measures that directly address clean water, wetland preservation, open space and recreation, and drainage patterns. The county succeeds in incorporating some mitigation measures in the form of auxiliary goals like prohibiting development in moderate- to high-quality wetlands and promoting only open space and recreational uses in flood zones. The county and the general plan need to address directly the fact that parts of the community are in the floodplain and that the dams, currently credited with mitigating flooding, may rupture or be breached (Figure 8.10). To the county's credit, meetings are being held to discuss this possibility. Also, the state is completing a dam breach assessment.

Interagency Cooperation. In addition to including mitigation in multiple goals, topics, and chapters, the plan creates the opportunity for diverse agencies in the county and region to work collaboratively.

- *Establish a monthly interagency plan review meeting.* Multiple agencies review and comment on proposed development plans.

- *Coordinate minimum fire-safety standards among local fire districts and wildland fire districts.* Compare building-code requirements, emergency vehicular ingress and egress access, response times, and fire-resistant landscaping in efforts to collaborate, sharing established best practices.

- *Implement procedures so Public Safety Department can offer input on all planning projects.*

Implementation Tools

The planning department is successfully implementing many objectives from the general plan that promote mitigation through the creation of a sensitive area district and adoption of a geologic hazards ordinance and subdivision

Figure 8.10. *In this map showing Morgan County dam inundation risk, the dam inundation areas are at top left, near the red dots indicating high-hazard dams.*

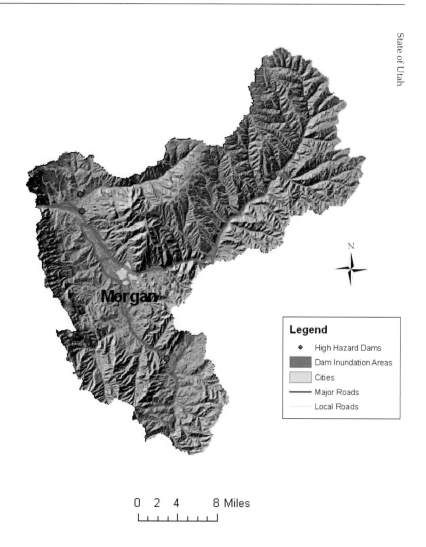

State of Utah

design standards and regulations. All of these include mandatory technical reports, mitigation action plans, suggestions for improvement beyond the requirements, the involvement of multiple departments, and funding sources. These are the policies and procedures that realize the goals and objectives supporting the community vision.

Sensitive Area District. The purpose of the Sensitive Area District is to permit the use of property while requiring design solutions that avoid negative impacts on sensitive natural areas and provide protection from adverse natural forces and hazards. Development in geologic hazard areas must:

- Have access roads to building lots free of geologic hazard

- Not build on fault scarps

- Not allow public improvements in landslide areas unless properly stabilized and paid for by the developer

- Address on each site within a subdivision:
  - Debris flow hazards, including past and future estimates
  - Slope stability, including static and dynamic conditions

- Be reviewed by the county planner, engineer, or building official, but applicants may request a third-party review, paid for by the developer

Utah Geological Survey

Figure 8.11. *Quartet of photos depicts aspects of Creekside landslide*

Subdivision Design and Regulations. General:

- In areas where topography limits safe access to public rights-of-way or where environmental damage and erosion need to be mitigated, residences are permitted to share driveways, serving up to four homes so as to provide an ingress and egress point safe from landslides. The slope of these driveways is regulated according to driveway length.

- The susceptibility of public utilities to damage from high winds, fire, earthquakes, and ice is a concern. Morgan County requires utilities to be buried in new subdivisions, and the developer is responsible for their installation. This serves to minimize public funding of development in new, possibly more costly areas and also to discourage developers from expanding into hazardous areas.

- Developers must include in the concept plan a soils and geologic map displaying hazards, stormwater disposal facilities, and a preliminary environmental impact assessment.

Fire:

- Development will not be approved if it would hinder firefighting or emergency-service capabilities due to its location or proximity to notable fire hazards (e.g., size, building materials, vegetation).

Flooding:

- No development is permitted in the floodway except gravel roads.

- All sewers and water systems in flood hazard areas must be installed or replaced with systems that minimize possible damage, including discharge and infiltration during a flooding event.

- All subdivisions must guarantee that the lowest floor of the building, including the basement, is constructed at least one foot above the 100-year base-flood elevation. In high-water-table areas, basements may be prohibited.

- A geotechnical engineer must investigate the groundwater impacts from development. Under no circumstances shall groundwater discharge into sanitary sewers, which would require increased storage and treatment.

Seismic:

- The Sensitive Land Regulations reinforce all the regulations introduced. A subdivision or a lot that is located on or adjacent to a fault line or escarpment must have two or more access roads. The zone of deformation, which is a nonbuildable area, must be marked on the design plat in red one-inch letters as "EQ HAZARD AREA."

Geologic Hazards Ordinance. The county found "compelling, countervailing public interest" to develop this ordinance. It specifically identifies three subdivisions with known geologic hazards and replaces a controversial building moratorium with new regulations and review for permits. All property owners in the identified areas seeking a building permit for a single dwelling on an already approved lot must complete a geologic hazard report. The following requirements apply:

- An engineering geologist must identify all hazards and recommend how to mitigate them on the property, if it is possible to do so.

- The owner must submit the report, including a mitigation plan, to two separate groups of reviewers:
  - The county engineer, planner, or building official
  - The Geologic Peer Review Board (GPRB), which is staffed by three professionals (e.g., engineering geologists, geotechnical engineers, or other qualified persons).

  The cost of the peer review is paid out of a $5,000 deposit the property owner makes at the start of the review process. While this creates the opportunity for landowners to prove their land is developable or properly mitigated, it makes them seriously consider whether there is less hazardous—and less expensive—land on which to build.

- If the GPRB grants a building permit, the owner must use the original engineering geologist to demonstrate construction compliance. For the final certification of occupancy, the owner must provide a Letter of Accordance from the engineering geologist.

- The owner is to run a notice with the land indicating that the parcel is in a geologic hazards area and that a report is on file with the county.

Lessons

All government officials, planners among them, assume the responsibility to keep a community safe. In light of Morgan County's hazards, the planning department works to protect residents without jeopardizing property owners' rights. With a limited tax base, it must minimize mitigation program costs. While Morgan County's actions are not the most innovative, they address all possible local hazards through a variety of tools and are able to make connections between the community's vision and hazard mitigation. As Morgan County has discovered, hazard mitigation planning is not easy, straightforward, or always seemingly rational; the reality is that complications appear at every turn. Looking into the future, a more effective and less costly way to mitigate the impact of the county's landslide activity is to prohibit platting land in any high-risk area. The ultimate mitigation tool is not an engineered mitigation plan but the analysis of whether development should happen at all.

CHAPTER 9

Findings and Recommendations

James C. Schwab, AICP

 Hazards of any kind—natural or otherwise—are almost never the public's top planning priority except when a disaster is unfolding. It is far easier to focus on any number of issues affecting the daily quality of life in a community, including economic development, transportation, and what is built next to what or whom. The reality, however, is that hazards suffuse our lives and our development patterns. They inevitably constitute part of the background for many of the other priorities planners must address and should be a consideration when those issues are on the table. Ignoring them does not make them go away. Consequently, finding ways to integrate the consideration of hazards into routine planning discussions is the most effective way to ensure that they are addressed when the community is in the best position to forestall problems.

This chapter summarizes the upshot of the research in this report: what works, what does not work, and lessons for the road ahead that will lead to safer communities.

WHAT WORKS?

Complementary Goals and Objectives in the Local Hazard Mitigation Plan and Comprehensive Plan

The best planning almost always starts out with clearly stated goals and objectives, understandable both to decision makers and the broader public. However, confusion can ensue in the treatment of hazards when the goals in one plan do not support those in the other or when the goals in a hazard mitigation plan are absent from the comprehensive plan. In addition, the hazard mitigation plan lacks the legal standing as a reference point for local land-development regulations that the comprehensive plan typically possesses. The signal, whether subtle or blatant, when coordination of plans is absent is that a community may not be treating hazards as a planning priority, especially in land-use planning. The best way to change that signal is to establish clear references in community plans to programs and planning activities addressing hazards and to use a hazards or safety element in the comprehensive plan and the local hazard mitigation plan to reinforce each other—something achieved in both Lee County, Florida, and Berkeley, California. Some communities have even used their hazard mitigation plan as an annex or appendix to the comprehensive plan.

Implementing Hazard Mitigation through Government Expenditures and Development Regulations

Even a comprehensive plan means nothing unless accompanied by some means of implementing its goals and objectives. This is most often achieved through public investment and by making and enforcing rules governing development. Goals and objectives that seek to minimize a community's exposure to hazards most often need one or both of these types of implementation support. Bourne, Massachusetts, made its hazard mitigation study a go-to document for developers and the general public seeking information and strategies concerning local hazards, thus amplifying its importance for planning activities. Development regulations provide some teeth for enforcing a community's decision to steer development away from hazardous areas. Allocating money for mitigation projects in the capital improvements or other capital budgeting program ensures that public investment is directed toward mitigating existing hazards. These investments can include the numerous property elevation, structural elevation, and flood control improvements implemented in Roseville, California; transportation improvements to provide more secure roads and bridges in the face of landslide and seismic hazards; and even safe rooms in public facilities in communities subject to tornadoes and windstorms.

Documenting Existing and Predicted Future Conditions and Raising Awareness of What Can Be Done about Them

Perhaps the most dramatic example of this principle is the use of build-out analysis by Charlotte and Mecklenburg County, North Carolina, to determine how growth under the existing zoning code would affect floodplain boundaries, flood elevations, and consequent damage patterns in future floods. Such innovative planning helps decision makers and the public connect the dots between the current situation and a less well-understood future, making it possible to agree on corrective measures to reshape development patterns. However, that initiative came from Storm Water Services and served as an input for reactive mitigation. Planners there did not seize the opportunity to fully integrate this information into the larger planning process, including both comprehensive and area plans and scenario analysis for proactive mitigation, nor did they play an integral part in the hazard mitigation planning process. Equally important, hazard mitigation officials failed to bring planners into the process of hazard mitigation planning. Mutual engagement could have made a great step forward even greater.

Mutual Reinforcement Between Hazard Mitigation and Other Planning Goals

Hazard mitigation shares essential values with many other planning goals that may prove mutually beneficial in terms of providing financial support or political will or both. Examples include public land acquisition or conservation easements for parks and open space in hazard-prone areas where allowing development would be more problematic. These actions tend to buttress the political support for hazard mitigation with support for the objectives involved. In Bourne and Roseville, the most effective tie seems to have been with economic development. Objective circumstances demand that making a community safe for investment is a literal proposition involving real hazard reduction through a variety of public mitigation strategies. In these cases, contrary to often-stated fears concerning development regulations, hazard mitigation is not a threat to investment but a welcome mat, giving investors greater confidence in the outcome. Much the same could be said of developer involvement in the future land-use mapping undertaken in Charlotte/Mecklenburg County.

Sustaining Leadership for Hazard Mitigation

Most cases of successful integration of hazard mitigation into local planning activities require the commitment of political leaders and local champions to sensible priorities for hazard mitigation. Invariably, someone or some group needs to exert leadership on the issue in order to enlist public support. In Berkeley, Lee County, and Roseville, leaders frequently pressed an agenda that could have lain dormant. In Bourne, the commitment of the town planner ensured creation of a local hazard mitigation plan when the opportunity arose, and the local economic development corporation's backing of the issue has given hazard mitigation a greater audience than it had before. Over time, the assumption of this mantle can become more routine and predictable, though never entirely guaranteed. But consistent leadership does tend to build political will in the long run.

Strong Culture of Preparedness and Mitigation

One result of consistent leadership can be the gradual development of a strong local or regional culture of preparedness and mitigation. Once the public accepts hazard mitigation and preparedness as essential elements of civic culture—as seems to have happened in Roseville and Bourne—other benefits flow from that cultural change. Berkeley has such a culture, which presumably makes it easier to learn about and accept challenging realities concerning local hazards. It has converted this public determination into forward-looking policies in its general plan to address hazards in its land-use planning. In a similar vein, Bourne seems to have accepted the need to mitigate local flood hazards under less-than-ideal circumstances.

Using External Drivers As Leverage While Focusing on Community Needs

State and federal laws contain a number of incentives and mandates for addressing hazards. These include the Disaster Mitigation Act of 2000 and other provisions of the Stafford Act, state planning and zoning enabling laws, and a host of other outside influences that may affect hazards. Planners can use these laws and programs to build local support for hazard mitigation and even to build a culture of preparedness and hazard mitigation. Planners can use incentives and requirements as justifications for giving hazards higher priority, and they can show how they increase local public safety. Certainly, the fact that DMA has induced almost 20,000 communities (as of March 2010) to adopt approved local hazard mitigation plans is substantial evidence that the carrot offered by the federal government—eligibility for hazard mitigation grants—has had significant influence on local behavior. The challenge for planners is to establish local capacity in such a way as to build local disaster resilience with the aid of such state and federal laws, rather than view them as yet another unfunded mandate.

Proactive Outreach and Stakeholder Involvement in Planning

A strong public culture of support for hazard mitigation depends on involvement. The best way to build involvement is through a proactive outreach program, aimed at key stakeholders, by both planners and allied professionals. Charlotte/Mecklenburg County demonstrated the strength of this approach when it incorporated future land-use projections into its floodplain mapping program. Local officials there strengthened public commitment to flood mitigation goals in large part by making sure that all parties understood how the information was derived and believed in the conclusions drawn from it. The case of Roseville demonstrates that another element of success in this regard is consistent, effective communication with the public. Berkeley further illustrates that, with the culture of preparedness and mitigation in place, widely shared public discussion of mitigation priorities allows citizens to preserve the best of their local community character while simultaneously achieving effective hazard mitigation.

WHAT DOES NOT WORK?

Procrastination

Postponing the confrontation with reality that hazard mitigation planning entails is simply unsound public policy. Tomorrow may be the day when an earthquake strikes, a flood inundates, or an unstable hillside tumbles and falls. More important, as the case of Lee County shows, even a comprehensive approach today cannot overturn years of unwise development. What has been built will remain until it is substantially remodeled, torn down, or destroyed in a disaster. For every community, today is the first day of the creation of the rest of its development pattern. Some of that pattern may involve redevelopment in existing built-out neighborhoods, but tragedy occurs when existing development proves unequal to the stresses of the next earthquake, hurricane, or flood. The best time to begin reshaping the current development pattern to create a more resilient community is now.

Failure to Involve Planners in Local Hazards Planning

When planners are not part of the process of preparing the local hazard mitigation plan, a serious disconnection occurs, reducing the likelihood of successful implementation. No one is at the table to discuss either the implications of hazard mitigation alternatives for land-use policy and planning or the effects of future land-use policies on community hazard vulnerability. Even if that plan is later incorporated into the comprehensive plan, the planning staff lacks the more intimate knowledge of the relationship of hazards to existing land use that would otherwise arise from their involvement from the outset. An entire series of other structural weaknesses in the local process of planning for hazard mitigation then flows from this initial mistake.

Failure to Engage Public Participation or to Communicate about Hazards

There are standards in the DMA approval process for public participation in the preparation of the local hazard mitigation plan. Federal standards are, however, a low common denominator; they are not the gold standard, which is being set by communities like Roseville, Berkeley, Bourne, and Charlotte. The goal is to build lasting public confidence in hazard mitigation as a meaningful and even essential priority for local planning. The public needs a sense of ownership of this priority, which can be achieved only through involvement from the outset and an atmosphere of open and honest communication.

Investment in Redevelopment without Accounting for Hazards

One reason for thorough integration of hazard mitigation into the plan implementation process is to ensure that hazards are considered in area redevelopment plans and in site plan reviews, as well as in any planning activity affecting the quality of development. The failure to account adequately for hazards when vulnerable areas are developed sets the stage for disaster losses. In most cases, the up-front costs of appropriate mitigation in the original scheme would have been far less than the later losses. The rapidly rising costs of disasters caused by natural hazards were the impetus for passage of DMA in 2000, *before* a decade of monstrous losses from disasters including hurricanes Rita, Katrina, and Ike; the Red River floods in North Dakota; floods in Iowa in 2008; and numerous major wildfires in Colorado, New Mexico, and California. After such losses, it is almost inconceivable that communities would want to take a step backward. Planners and local decision makers need to consider those sensibilities in local redevelopment decisions.

Failure to Use Other Plans to Address Hazards

As noted in Chapter 5, communities typically develop a number of other plans besides the comprehensive plan. All of these plans—downtown, neighborhood, corridor, sewage treatment, transit, and water-quality plans, just to name a few—present opportunities to address hazard mitigation, often in a manner that would support and serve multiple objectives. Many of them involve significant public investment, if not redevelopment, and the public is increasingly unlikely to be tolerant of seeing its investments squandered through a failure to contemplate the consequences of natural and other hazards.

THE ROAD AHEAD

This final section is a brief road map not only for communities but for national policy, not in the sense of prescribing specific policies but in suggesting a simple but broad set of principles for guiding policy development as it affects local planning.

Learn from Disasters

Disasters stemming from natural hazards are invariably cyclical—though, if anything, climate change is likely to worsen some of their impacts. The cycle may be long or short, depending on the severity and the nature of the hazard, but what has happened before can and *will* happen again. Unfortunately, it seems to be a part of human nature to try to avoid or ignore the implications of this truism. But good public policy is not written by ostriches. The communities studied here all benefited from the willingness of public leaders to help reorient public policy by absorbing the lessons of experience, as a way of steadily building increased resilience into community institutions, managerial structures, and development patterns. Recent efforts in Florida to adopt postdisaster redevelopment plans offer one way to institutionalize the means of distilling those lessons by anticipating the challenges a community may face after a disaster and how to gain the greatest wisdom from what happens. Postdisaster redevelopment plans and recovery ordinances, in addition to local hazard mitigation plans, should always incorporate provisions for assessing the lessons learned from each disaster.

Start Change Now

Starting now to build pressure for change is clearly the obverse of procrastinating. Even the voice crying in the wilderness eventually has some impact on public awareness, but planners and allied professionals are usually in good positions to make their case with decision makers, given an arsenal of scientific detail and the historic evidence of past failures to act responsibly. Planners also have ethical obligations to help protect public safety. One principle in the AICP code of ethics states: "We shall have special concern for the long-range consequences of present actions." Increasingly, modern knowledge of hazards underscores the salience of this responsibility, as Hurricane Katrina showed all too poignantly. Climate change and sea-level rise will serve only to heighten this responsibility. Carpe diem.

Strengthen Integration of Hazards with Other Planning Activities

This responsibility permeates policy making at all levels of government. At the federal level, FEMA has latitude within the Stafford Act and its DMA amendments to achieve changes that motivate local governments in this direction. With each wave of updates, it should be possible to prod local governments a little harder to consider how their local hazard mitigation plans relate to other aspects of policy making and how various agencies and stakeholders can be further involved in helping to achieve this integration. It is not the job of the federal government to prescribe exactly how this gets done, and as the case studies suggest there is considerable room at the local level for creativity in achieving this integration. It may also be time for FEMA to reduce its reliance on emergency management channels in favor of using a broader network of professionals. The lively precedent of the NFIP's Community Rating System suggests strongly that FEMA is capable of crafting creative incentives that work.

At the same time, state laws show considerable potential for encouraging greater integration of hazards with other planning activities. Already, 10 states require a hazards element in local comprehensive plans. It is not a large step from there to ensure that such elements could serve double duty as local hazard mitigation plans under DMA, by meeting both federal and state requirements or by requiring horizontal consistency between local hazard mitigation plans and comprehensive plans, just as they often require consistency between zoning and comprehensive plans. Since 1998, Florida has been encouraging local mitigation strategies that serve that purpose; California is also paying close attention to this issue. States are also in a position to provide technical assistance to local governments in crafting such plans and elements, and many provide significant technical assistance already, either generally or for specific hazards of statewide concern, such as the assistance of the Colorado State Forest Service with regard to wildfires and the provision of SLOSH maps for all of Florida based on high-quality Lidar elevation data. Moreover, regional planning agencies, which are typically creations of state government, are also in positions to provide such assistance. These agencies are often contracted to produce either single- or multijurisdictional hazard mitigation plans for local governments in various states. Working with local governments to pave the way toward greater integration of such plans with other local planning activities would be a perfectly logical step, and both state and regional officials could assist in moving plan preparation in that direction.

Ultimately, however, the political will for such integration must be found at the local level, through the champions and policy advocates and planners who are willing to move the issue forward. They must keep placing in the minds of decision makers the simple principle that public safety—not simply meeting minimum requirements for hazard mitigation grants—must be their ultimate priority.

Think Linkages

Creativity in many cases consists largely of associative thinking. It is a matter of discovering new connections between seemingly different ideas. It is realizing new ways to harness the strength of one idea to promote another. This report is ultimately all about establishing linkages among the often isolated plans for hazard mitigation and the everyday functions of most urban and regional planning. The way forward is to challenge ourselves to consider how the various parts of community planning may fit together in new ways to achieve goals valued by the entire community. The awards and accolades in planning tend to go to those individuals and communities who possess that creative streak and find new and imaginative ways to achieve those goals.

It is no surprise, then, that the small community of Greensburg, Kansas, captured the national imagination by combining reconstruction after a devastating EF-5 tornado with green building. Faced with a declining and aging population that was effectively homeless, civic leaders turned away from self-pity to embrace a grand vision of the future that combined a series of compelling public priorities in what can be called *green postdisaster redevelopment*. However, such redevelopment must include effective hazard mitigation in its principles, for there is nothing less green and more wasteful than destruction that did not need to happen. The point is not that Greensburg found the ultimate model for rebuilding after a disaster. Many of the circumstances are unique, as they always are. Green building initiatives have not yet always shown a great awareness of hazard mitigation. What is admirable is the willingness of local leaders to embrace a new combination of ideas; Greensburg's new Sustainable Comprehensive Plan (www .greensburgks.org/recovery-planning/Greensburg%20Comprehensive%20 Master%20Plan%2001-16-08%20DRAFT.pdf) is nothing if not a blueprint for further creative thinking.

Community leaders need to think holistically about planning for hazards, identify opportunities and resources to achieve their goals, treat mitigation as an investment in protection of public and private investments, and seek synergies that achieve those results in the most cost-effective ways possible. Focusing on *thinking linkages* is perhaps the most exciting and potent way to get there.

References

Alesch, Daniel J. n.d. "A Critical Role: Top Ten Policies That States Need to Recover from Disasters." Washington, D.C.: U.S. Chamber of Commerce, Business Civic Leadership Council. Available at www.uschamber.com/bclc/programs/disaster/statepolicyclusters.htm.

Alesch, Daniel J., Lucy A. Arendt, and James N. Holly. 2008. *Managing for Long-term Community Recovery in the Aftermath of Disaster*. Fairfax, Va.: Public Entity Risk Institute.

American Forests. 2003. *Urban Ecosystem Analysis: Mecklenburg County, North Carolina*. Washington, D.C.: American Forests.

Beatley, Timothy. 2009. *Planning for Coastal Resilience: Best Practices for Calamitous Times*. Washington, D.C.: Island Press. Chapter 6, 59–71.

Berkeley, California, City of. 2001. *General Plan: A Guide for Public Decision-Making*. December.

———. 2004. *Disaster Mitigation Plan*. June.

Boswell, Michael, K. Topping, W. Siembieda, et al. 2008. *Local Hazard Mitigation Planning in California*, A Report on the Implementation of LHMPs under DMA 2000. Sacramento: California Governor's Office of Emergency Services.

Bourne, Massachusetts, Town of. 2004. *Pre-Disaster Hazard Mitigation Plan*. October 21. Available at www.townofbourne.com/LinkClick.aspx?fileticket=SQ3SczQbi%2fQ%3d&tabid=177&mid=795.

———. 2006. *Local Comprehensive Plan*. Updated 2008. Available at www.townofbourne.com/LinkClick.aspx?fileticket=6vI%2fDV18IWU%3d&tabid=177&mid=1349.

———. 2009. *Zoning Bylaw*. Section II, Use and Intensity Regulations. Part 2800. Downtown District. Section III, General Regulations. Part 3110. Lowland Regulations–Flood Area Provisions. Available at www.townofbourne.com/LinkClick.aspx?fileticket=VqANHXqTGg0%3d&tabid=177&mid=1349.

Brovitz, Ted. 2009. Associate Planner, Stantec Planning and Landscape Architecture. Telephone conversation with Ann Dillemuth, May 8.

Burban, Lisa L., and John W. Andresen. 1994. *Storms over the Urban Forest*. 2d ed. St. Paul, Minn.: USDA Forest Service, Northeastern Area.

Burby, Raymond J. 2005. "Have State Comprehensive Planning Mandates Reduced Insured Losses from Natural Disasters?" *Natural Hazards Review* 6(2): 67–81.

———. 2006. "Hurricane Katrina and the Paradoxes of Government Disaster Policy: Bringing about Wise Governmental Decisions for Hazardous Areas." *The Annals of the American Academy of Political and Social Science* 604(1): 171–91.

Burby, Raymond J., Robert E. Deyle, David R. Godschalk, and Robert B. Olshansky. 2000. "Creating Hazard-resilient Communities through Land-use Planning." *Natural Hazards Review* 1(2): 99–106. May.

Burby, Raymond J., Arthur C. Nelson, Dennis Parker, and John Handmer. 2001. "Urban Containment Policy and Exposure to Natural Hazards: Is There a Connection?" *Journal of Environmental Planning and Management* 44(4): 475–90. July.

Burrows, Julia. 2009. Deputy City Manager, City of Roseville. Interview with Kenneth C. Topping. March 17.

California Department of Water Resources. 2007. Delta Emergency Operations Plan—Concept Paper. April. Sacramento: California Department of Water Resources.

California Governor's Office of Emergency Services (OES). 2007. *2007 State of California Multi-Hazard Mitigation Plan.* Available at http://hazardmit igation.oes.ca.gov/plan/state_multi-hazard_mitigation_plan_shmp.

Charlotte-Mecklenburg [North Carolina] Planning Department. 2007. *General Development Policies.* Available at www.charmeck.org/Departments/Planning/Area+Planning/Plans/GDP/home.htm.

———. 2008. *Centers, Corridors and Wedges: Growth Framework–Draft.* Available at www.charmeck.org/Departments/Planning/Area+Planning/Centers+Corridors+and+Wedges/Home.htm.

Charlotte-Mecklenburg [North Carolina] Storm Water Services. 1997. *Mecklenburg County Floodplain Guidance Management Document.* Available at www.charmeck.org/Departments/StormWater/Storm+Water+Professionals/Master+Plans+and+Long+Term+Strategies.htm.

———. 2007. *Post-Construction Stormwater Ordinance.* Available at www.charmeck.org/Departments/StormWater/Contractors/PCSWO+Mecklenburg+County+and+Towns.htm.

Christensen, Sherrie. 2008. Community Development Director, Morgan County. Telephone conversation with Rebecca Little. December 29.

Dennison, Mark S. 1996. "Zoning and the Comprehensive Plan." *Zoning News.* August, 1–4.

Deyle, Robert, Timothy Chapin, and Earl Baker. 2008. "The Proof of the Planning Is in the Platting." *Journal of the American Planning Association* 74(3): 349–70.

Deyle, Robert E., and Richard A. Smith. 1994. *Storm Hazard Mitigation and Post-Storm Redevelopment Policies.* Report of a Project to the Coastal Zone Management Program, Florida Department of Community Affairs (Contract No. 930S-07-13-00-15-012). Tallahassee: Florida Planning Laboratory, Department of Urban and Regional Planning, Florida State University.

Eadie, Charles D. 1998. "Earthquake Case Study: Loma Prieta in Santa Cruz and Watsonville, California." In Schwab et al. 1998.

Federal Emergency Management Agency (FEMA). 2001–2003. "Mitigation Planning 'How-To' Guides." Ten guides available online, in print, and as CD-ROM. Washington, D.C.: FEMA. Available online at www.fema.gov/plan/mitplanning/resources.shtm.

———. 2003. *Integrating Manmade Hazards into Mitigation Planning*. State and Local Mitigation Planning How-to Guide no. 7. September.

———. 2007. *Principles of Emergency Management Supplement*. September 11. Available online at http://training.fema.gov/EMIWeb/edu/emprinciples.asp.

———. 2009. "State Multi-Hazard Mitigation Planning Guidance." Available at www.fema.gov/library/viewRecord.do?id=3115.

Firewise Communities. 2009. *Safer from the Start: A Guide to Firewise-Friendly Developments*. Quincy, Mass.: National Fire Protection Association.

Florida, State of. n.d. *The Local Mitigation Strategy: A Guide for Florida Cities and Counties*. Available at www.floridadisaster.org/BRM/LMS/LMS%20Guiding%20Principles.htm.

Florida Department of Community Affairs (DCA) and Department of Agriculture and Consumer Services (DACS). 2004. *Wildfire Mitigation in Florida: Land Use Planning Strategies and Best Development Practices*. Tallahassee: Florida DCA and Florida DACS. April. Available at www.dca.state.fl.us/fdcp/DCP/publications/Files/Wildfire_Mitigation_in_FL.pdf.

Florida DCA, Division of Community Planning and Division of Emergency Management. 2006. *Protecting Florida's Communities: Land Use Planning and Best Development Practices for Minimizing Vulnerability to Flooding and Coastal Storms*. Tallahassee: Florida DCA. September. Available at www.dca.state.fl.us/fdcp/DCP/publications/Files/hazmitbp.pdf.

Florida Department of State, Florida Department of Community Affairs, and 1000 Friends of Florida. 2006. *Disaster Planning for Florida's Historic Resources*. Tallahassee: 1000 Friends of Florida. May. Available at www.1000friendsofflorida.org/PUBS/HistoricalDisater/1000%20Friends%20Book.pdf.

Freudenburg, William R., Robert B. Gramling, Shirley Laska, and Kai Ericson. 2009. *Catastrophe in the Making: The Engineering of Katrina and the Disasters of Tomorrow*. Washington, D.C.: Shearwater.

Galloway, Gerald E. 1995. "Learning from the Mississippi Flood of 1993: Impacts, Management Issues, and Areas for Research." Perugia, Italy: U.S.–Italy Research Workshop on the Hydrometeorology, Impacts, and Management of Extreme Floods. November.

Godschalk, David. 2007. "Mitigation." Pp. 89–112 in *Emergency Management: Principles and Practice for Local Government*, 2d ed., ed. W. Waugh and K. Tierney. Washington, D.C.: ICMA Press.

———. 2009. "Safe Growth Audits." *Zoning Practice*. September.

Godschalk, David, David Brower, and Timothy Beatley. 1989. *Catastrophic Coastal Storms: Hazard Mitigation and Development Management*. Durham, N.C.: Duke University Press.

Godschalk, David R., Adam Rose, Elliott Mittler, Keith Porter, and Carol Taylor West. 2009. "Estimating the Value of Foresight: Aggregate Analysis of Natural Hazard Mitigation Benefits and Costs." *Journal of Environmental Planning and Management* 52(6): 739–56.

Greensburg, Kansas, City of, and BNIM Architects. 2008. *Greensburg Sustainable Comprehensive Plan*. Available online at www.greensburgks .org/recovery-planning/Greensburg%20Comprehensive%20Master%20 Plan%2001-16-08%20DRAFT.pdf.

Institute for Business and Home Safety (IBHS). 2009. "Summary of State Land Use and Natural Hazards Planning Laws, 2008." Available at www .disastersafety.org/publications/view.asp?id=8021.

Justus, Stacey. 2009. Former Coastal Resources Specialist, Cape Cod Commission. Telephone conversation with Ann Dillemuth, March 10.

Kane County, Illinois. 2003. *Natural Hazards Mitigation Plan*. Available at www.co.kane.il.us/hazards/finalPlan/execsum.pdf and www.co.kane .il.us/hazards/finalPlan/toc.pdf.

Kansas Office of the Governor and Federal Emergency Management Agency (FEMA) Region VII. 2007. *Long-Term Community Recovery Plan: Greensburg + Kiowa County, Kansas*. August. Washington, D.C.: FEMA.

Kennen, Kate. 2009. Landscape Architect, Kennen Landscape Architecture. Telephone conversation with Ann Dillemuth, April 6.

Kennen Landscape Architecture with Ocean-US Design and Coastal Engineering Company. 2007. *Study of Flood Hazard Mitigation and Design for the Main Street Business District, Village of Buzzards Bay, MA*. Available at www .bfdconline.org/pdf/Flood%20Study%20Final%20Report.pdf.

Kent, T. J. *The Urban General Plan*. 1964. San Francisco: Chandler.

Kollin, Cheryl. 2009. "McDowell Creek Watershed, North Carolina." Pp. 103–11 in Schwab, ed., 2009.

Kusler, Jon A. 2009. "A Comparative Look at Public Liability for Flood Hazard Mitigation." Prepared for the Association of State Floodplain Managers Foundation. Available at www.floods.org/PDF/Mitigation/ASFPM _Comparative_look_at_pub_liability_for_flood_haz_mitigation_09.pdf.

Larson, Larry. 2003. Statement at Natural Hazards Workshop, Boulder, Colo. July 15.

Laughlin, Brian. 2009. "Roseville Flood Mitigation," unpublished paper. June.

Lee County Board of County Commissioners [Florida]. 2007. *Lee County Master Mitigation Plan (Environmental Quality Investment and Growth Mitigation Strategic Plan)*. Available at www.swfrpc.org/content/Publication/ LMMP.pdf.

Lee County Department of Community Development (DCD). 2008. Letter to Daniel DeLisi re: North River Village. Available at www.alvafl.org/ Files/Lee%20Staff%20%20letter%20to%20Bonita%20Bay%20Group%20 re%20North%20River%20Village.pdf.

———. 2009a. *The Lee Plan*. Available at www3.leegov.com/dcd1/Leeplan/ Leeplan.pdf.

Lee County Division of Emergency Management. 2007. *Hazard Vulnerability Analysis*. Available at www.leeeoc.com/aboutus/vulnerabilityanalysis .aspx.

Local Mitigation Strategy Work Group. 2007. *Joint Unified Local Mitigation Strategy for Lee County, Florida*. Available at www.fortmyersbeachfl.gov/ FMB/CouncilPackets/04-21-08/TC042108buVB.pdf.

Lucy, William. 1988. *Close to Power: Setting Priorities with Elected Officials.* Chicago: APA Planners Press.

Malin, Craig Thomas. 2009. "Innovative Floodplain Management." Presentation at APA National Planning Conference, Minneapolis. April 27. Available via www.planning.org/conference/previous/2009/digital capture.htm.

McKibben, Bill. 1989. *The End of Nature.* New York: Random House.

Mead, T. D. 2000. "Governing Charlotte-Mecklenburg." *State and Local Government Review* 32(3): 192–97.

Meck, Stuart, ed. 2002. *Growing Smart Legislative Guidebook: Model Statutes for Planning and the Management of Change.* Chicago: American Planning Association.

Mecklenburg County Emergency Management (MCEM). 2005. *Mecklenburg County Multi-Jurisdictional Hazard Mitigation Plan.* Available at www .charmeck.org/Departments/StormWater/Storm+Water+Professionals/ Master+Plans+and+Long+Term+Strategies.htm.

Mecklenburg County Department of Parks and Recreation. 2008. *Greenway Plan Update.* Available at www.charmeck.org/Departments/ Park+and+Rec/Greenways/Home.htm.

Moore, Coreen. 2009. Town Planner, Town of Bourne, Massachusetts. Telephone conversation with Ann Dillemuth, February 20.

Morgan, Utah, County of. 2007. *1999 Morgan County General Plan.* Amended May.

National Research Council. 1990. *Managing Coastal Erosion.* Washington, D.C.: National Academy Press.

New Orleans, City of. 2009. *A Plan for the 21st Century: New Orleans 2030.* Available at www.nolamasterplan.org.

Nolon, John R. 2007. "The Quiet Revolution in Training Citizen Planners." *Zoning Practice.* April, 2–7.

North Carolina Emergency Management Division (NCEMD). 2000. *Hazard Mitigation in North Carolina: Measuring Success.* Raleigh, N.C.: NCEMD.

Perry, Ronald W., and Michael K. Lindell. 2007. *Emergency Planning.* Hoboken, N.J.: John Wiley and Sons.

Pielke, R. A. 2005. "Land Use and Climate Change." *Science* 310(9): 1625–26.

Pilkey, Orrin H, Jr., William J. Neal, Orrin H. Pilkey Sr., and Stanley R. Riggs. 1980. *From Currituck to Calabash: Living with North Carolina's Barrier Islands.* Durham, N.C.: Duke University Press.

Pilkey, Orrin H, Jr., William J. Neal, Stanley R. Riggs, Craig A. Webb, David M. Bush, Deborah F. Pilkey, Jane Bullock, and Brian A. Cowan. 1998. *The North Carolina Shore and Its Barrier Islands: Restless Ribbons of Sand.* Durham, N.C.: Duke University Press.

Platt, Rutherford. 1999. *Disasters and Democracy: The Politics of Extreme Natural Events.* Washington, D.C.: Island Press.

Pyne, Stephen J. 1982. *Fire in America: A Cultural History of Wildland and Rural Fire.* Princeton, N.J.: Princeton University Press.

Rehm, Ronald G., Anthony Hamins, Howard R. Baum, Kevin B. McGrattan, and David D. Evans. 2002. "Community-Scale Fire Spread." NISTIR 6891. Available at http://fire.nist.gov/bfrlpubs/fire02/PDF/f02019.pdf.

Riggs, Sallie. 2009. Executive Director, Bourne Financial Development Corporation. Telephone conversation with Ann Dillemuth, March 18.

Rose, Adam, et al. 2007. "Benefit-Cost Analysis of FEMA Hazard Mitigation Grants." *Natural Hazards Review*. November.

Roseville, California, City of. 2005a *Hazard Mitigation Plan*. June. Available online at www.roseville.ca.us/fire/emergency_preparedness/multi_haz ard_mitigation_plan.asp.

———. 2005b. Roseville 2020 General Plan Safety Element. Available online at www.roseville.ca.us/civica/filebank/blobdload.asp?BlobID=2546.

Schwab, Anna K., Katherine Eschelbach, and David J. Brower. 2007. *Hazard Mitigation and Preparedness*. Hoboken, N.J.: John Wiley and Sons.

Schwab, James. 2004. "Planning for a Rainy Day: Addressing Natural Hazards in State Land-Use Laws." *Planning and Environmental Law* 56(1): 3–8.

———. 2009. "Winds of Change." *Planning*. October, 24–29.

Schwab, James, ed. 2009. *Planning the Urban Forest: Ecology, Economy, and Community Development*. Planning Advisory Service Report No. 555. Chicago: APA.

Schwab, James, and Stuart Meck, with Jamie Simone. 2005. *Planning for Wildfires*. Planning Advisory Service Report No. 529/530. Chicago: APA.

Schwab, James, with Kenneth C. Topping, Charles D. Eadie, Robert E. Deyle, and Richard A. Smith. 1998. *Planning for Post-Disaster Recovery and Reconstruction*. Planning Advisory Service Report No. 483/484. Chicago: American Planning Association.

Smith, G. 2008. "Planning for Sustainable and Disaster Resilient Communities." Pp. 221–48 in J. Pine, *Natural Hazards Analysis: Reducing the Impact of Disasters*. New York: Auerbach.

Stantec Planning and Landscape Architecture. 2008. *A Vision Plan for Bourne's Downtown: The Village of Buzzards Bay*. Available at www.bfdconline.org/Vision-for-Bourne.php.

Thomas, Edward A., and Sam Riley Medlock. 2008. "Mitigating Misery: Land Use and Protection of Property Rights before the Next Flood." *Vermont Journal of Environmental Law* 9(2): 155–88.

Tobin, Graham A., and Burrell E. Montz. 1997. "Public Policy and Natural Hazards." Pp. 196–244 in *Natural Hazards: Explanation and Integration*. New York: Guilford Press.

Topping, Kenneth C. 2006. "A New Approach to Earthquake Disaster Risk Reduction Planning in the U.S.: Lessons from the Disaster Mitigation Act of 2000." Proceedings of the Second Asian Council on Earthquake Engineering Conference, Manila, Philippines. March.

Trautman, Tim. 2009. Program Manager, Mecklenburg County Flood Mitigation. Personal correspondence with Joseph MacDonald. May 18.

Turner, A. Keith, and Robert L. Schuster, eds. 1996. *Landslides: Investigation and Mitigation*. Transportation Research Board, National Research Council, Special Report 247. Washington, D.C.: National Academy Press.

Unified New Orleans Plan. 2007. Composite of plans for 13 planning districts, available at www.unifiedneworleansplan.com/home3.

U.S. Government Accountability Office (GAO). 2005. *Continuity of Operations: Agency Plans Have Improved, but Better Oversight Could Assist Agencies in Preparing for Emergencies*. GAO-05-577. April. Washington, D.C.: GAO.

———. 2007. *Natural Hazard Mitigation: Various Mitigation Efforts Exist, but Federal Efforts Do Not Provide a Comprehensive Strategic Framework*. GAO-07-403. Washington, D.C.: GAO.

Waddington, Lynda. 2009. "Flood Victims, Officials Discuss Recovery in Cedar Rapids." *Iowa Independent*. August 13. Available at http://iowaindependent.com/18555/flood-victims-officials-discuss-recovery-in-cedar-rapids.

Walther, Lincoln N. 2009. "What's the Latest in Hazard Planning?" *Florida Planning*. June, 1, 5.

Wasatch Front Regional Council. 2003. *Natural Hazard Pre-Disaster Mitigation Plan*. Available online at www.wfrc.org/cms/index.php?option=com_content&task=view&id=102&Itemid=38.

White, Sarah. 2009. Hazard Mitigation Planner, Massachusetts Emergency Management Agency. Telephone conversation with Ann Dillemuth, September 8.

Witten, Jon D. 2006. "Critical and Sensitive Areas Plans." Pp. 41–42 in *Planning and Urban Design Standards*. Hoboken, N.J.: John Wiley and Sons.

Yang, Heloisa, Matt Haynes, Stephen Winzenread, and Kevin Okada. 1999. "The History of Dams." Available at http://cee.engr.ucdavis.edu/faculty/lund/dams/Dam_History_Page/History.htm.

Zagzebski, Kathy. 2009. President and Executive Director, National Marine Life Center. Telephone conversation with Ann Dillemuth, March 13.

American Planning Association

Making Great Communities Happen

The American Planning Association provides leadership in the development of vital communities by advocating excellence in community planning, promoting education and citizen empowerment, and providing the tools and support necessary to effect positive change.

515. Planning for Street Connectivity: Getting from Here to There. Susan Handy, Robert G. Paterson, and Kent Butler. May 2003. 95pp.

516. Jobs-Housing Balance. Jerry Weitz. November 2003. 41pp.

517. Community Indicators. Rhonda Phillips. December 2003. 46pp.

518/519. Ecological Riverfront Design. Betsy Otto, Kathleen McCormick, and Michael Leccese. March 2004. 177pp.

520. Urban Containment in the United States. Arthur C. Nelson and Casey J. Dawkins. March 2004. 130pp.

521/522. A Planners Dictionary. Edited by Michael Davidson and Fay Dolnick. April 2004. 460pp.

523/524. Crossroads, Hamlet, Village, Town (revised edition). Randall Arendt. April 2004. 142pp.

525. E-Government. Jennifer Evans–Cowley and Maria Manta Conroy. May 2004. 41pp.

526. Codifying New Urbanism. Congress for the New Urbanism. May 2004. 97pp.

527. Street Graphics and the Law. Daniel Mandelker with Andrew Bertucci and William Ewald. August 2004. 133pp.

528. Too Big, Boring, or Ugly: Planning and Design Tools to Combat Monotony, the Too-big House, and Teardowns. Lane Kendig. December 2004. 103pp.

529/530. Planning for Wildfires. James Schwab and Stuart Meck. February 2005. 126pp.

531. Planning for the Unexpected: Land-Use Development and Risk. Laurie Johnson, Laura Dwelley Samant, and Suzanne Frew. February 2005. 59pp.

532. Parking Cash Out. Donald C. Shoup. March 2005. 119pp.

533/534. Landslide Hazards and Planning. James C. Schwab, Paula L. Gori, and Sanjay Jeer, Project Editors. September 2005. 209pp.

535. The Four Supreme Court Land-Use Decisions of 2005: Separating Fact from Fiction. August 2005. 193pp.

536. Placemaking on a Budget: Improving Small Towns, Neighborhoods, and Downtowns Without Spending a Lot of Money. Al Zelinka and Susan Jackson Harden. December 2005. 133pp.

537. Meeting the Big Box Challenge: Planning, Design, and Regulatory Strategies. Jennifer Evans–Crowley. March 2006. 69pp.

538. Project Rating/Recognition Programs for Supporting Smart Growth Forms of Development. Douglas R. Porter and Matthew R. Cuddy. May 2006. 51pp.

539/540. Integrating Planning and Public Health: Tools and Strategies To Create Healthy Places. Marya Morris, General Editor. August 2006. 144pp.

541. An Economic Development Toolbox: Strategies and Methods. Terry Moore, Stuart Meck, and James Ebenhoh. October 2006. 80pp.

542. Planning Issues for On-site and Decentralized Wastewater Treatment. Wayne M. Feiden and Eric S. Winkler. November 2006. 61pp.

543/544. Planning Active Communities. Marya Morris, General Editor. December 2006. 116pp.

545. Planned Unit Developments. Daniel R. Mandelker. March 2007. 140pp.

546/547. The Land Use/Transportation Connection. Terry Moore and Paul Thorsnes, with Bruce Appleyard. June 2007. 440pp.

548. Zoning as a Barrier to Multifamily Housing Development. Garrett Knaap, Stuart Meck, Terry Moore, and Robert Parker. July 2007. 80pp.

549/550. Fair and Healthy Land Use: Environmental Justice and Planning. Craig Anthony Arnold. October 2007. 168pp.

551. From Recreation to Re-creation: New Directions in Parks and Open Space System Planning. Megan Lewis, General Editor. January 2008. 132pp.

552. Great Places in America: Great Streets and Neighborhoods, 2007 Designees. April 2008. 84pp.

553. Planners and the Census: Census 2010, ACS, Factfinder, and Understanding Growth. Christopher Williamson. July 2008. 132pp.

554. A Planners Guide to Community and Regional Food Planning: Transforming Food Environments, Facilitating Healthy Eating. Samina Raja, Branden Born, and Jessica Kozlowski Russell. August 2008. 112pp.

555. Planning the Urban Forest: Ecology, Economy, and Community Development. James C. Schwab, General Editor. January 2009. 160pp.

556. Smart Codes: Model Land-Development Regulations. Marya Morris, General Editor. April 2009. 260pp.

557. Transportation Infrastructure: The Challenges of Rebuilding America. Marlon G. Boarnet, Editor. July 2009. 128pp.

558. Planning for a New Energy and Climate Future. Scott Shuford, Suzanne Rynne, and Jan Mueller. February 2010. 160pp.

559. Complete Streets: Best Policy and Implementation Practices. Barbara McCann and Suzanne Rynne, Editors. March 2010. 144pp.

560. Hazard Mitigation: Integrating Best Practices into Planning. James C. Schwab, Editor. May 2010. 152pp.